HEIDEGGER FOR ARCHITECTS

Thinkers for Architects

Series Editor: Adam Sharr, Cardiff University, UK

Editorial Board

Jonathan A. Hale, University of Nottingham, UK

Hilde Heynen, KU Leuven, Netherlands

David Leatherbarrow, University of Pennsylvania, USA

Architects have often looked to philosophers and theorists from beyond the discipline for design inspiration or in search of a critical framework for practice. This original series offers quick, clear introductions to key thinkers who have written about architecture and whose work can yield insights for designers.

Deleuze and Guattari for Architects

Andrew Ballantyne

Heidegger for Architects

Adam Sharr

Irigaray for Architects

Peg Rawes

Heidegger

for

Architects

Adam Sharr

LONDON AND NEW YORK

First published 2007
by Routledge
2 Park Square, Milton Park, Abingdon, Oxon OX14 4RN

Simultaneously published in the USA and Canada
by Routledge
270 Madison Avenue, New York, NY 10016

Routledge is an imprint of the Taylor & Francis Group, an informa business

Typeset in Frutiger and Galliard by
Florence Production Ltd, Stoodleigh, Devon
Printed and bound in Great Britain by
The Cromwell Press, Trowbridge, Wiltshire

British Library Cataloguing in Publication Data
A catalogue record for this book is available from the British Library

Library of Congress Cataloging in Publication Data
Sharr, Adam.
  Heidegger for architects / Adam Sharr.
      p. cm. – (Thinkers for architects series)
   Includes bibliographical references and index.
   1. Heidegger, Martin, 1889–1976.   2. Architecture – Philosophy.
   I. Title.
   B3279.H49S423 2007
   193 – dc22   2007013320

ISBN10: 0–415–41515–2 (hbk)
ISBN10: 0–415–41517–9 (pbk)
ISBN10: 0–203–93419–9 (ebk)

ISBN13: 978–0–415–41515–6 (hbk)
ISBN13: 978–0–415–41517–0 (pbk)
ISBN13: 978–0–203–93419–7 (ebk)

For P.

Contents

Series Editor's Preface

Adam Sharr

Architects have often looked to thinkers in philosophy and theory for design ideas, or in search of a critical framework for practice. Yet architects and students of architecture can struggle to navigate thinkers' writings. It can be daunting to approach original texts with little appreciation of their contexts and existing introductions seldom explore architectural material in any detail. This original series offers clear, quick and accurate introductions to key thinkers who have written about architecture. Each book summarizes what a thinker has to offer for architects. It locates their architectural thinking in the body of their work, introduces significant books and essays, helps decode terms and provides quick reference for further reading. If you find philosophical and theoretical writing about architecture difficult, or just don't know where to begin, this series will be indispensable.

Books in the *Thinkers for Architects* series come out of architecture. They pursue architectural modes of understanding, aiming to introduce a thinker to an architectural audience. Each thinker has a unique and distinctive ethos, and the structure of each book derives from the character at its focus. The thinkers explored are prodigious writers and any short introduction can only address a fraction of their work. Each author – an architect or an architectural critic – has focused on a selection of a thinker's writings which they judge most relevant to designers and interpreters of architecture. Inevitably, much will be left out. These books will be the first point of reference, rather than the last word, about a particular thinker for architects. It is hoped that they will encourage you to read further; offering an incentive to delve deeper into the original writings of a particular thinker.

The first three books in the series explore the work of: Gilles Deleuze and Felix Guattari; Martin Heidegger; and Luce Irigaray. Familiar cultural figures, these are thinkers whose writings have already influenced architectural designers and critics in distinctive and important ways. It is hoped that this series will expand over time to cover a rich diversity of contemporary thinkers who have something to say to architects.

Adam Sharr is Senior Lecturer at the Welsh School of Architecture, Cardiff University, and Principal of Adam Sharr Architects. He is author of *Heidegger's Hut* (MIT Press, 2006), *Heidegger for Architects* (Routledge, 2007), joint editor of *Primitive: Original Matters in Architecture* (Routledge, 2006) and Associate Editor of *arq: Architectural Research Quarterly* (Cambridge University Press).

Illustration Credits

Peter Blundell-Jones, page 108; page 110.
David Dernie, page 93; page 94; page 102.
Digne Meller-Marcovicz, page xiv.
Adam Sharr, page 15; page 16; page 18; page 65.

Acknowledgements

Caroline Almond, Patrick Devlin, Mhairi McVicar and Joanne Sayner read drafts of this book and their comments were invaluable. Peter Blundell-Jones and David Dernie kindly provided photographs. Caroline Mallinder and Georgina Johnson from Routledge have generously supported both the book and the 'Thinkers for Architects' series. I'm indebted to friends, students and colleagues whose interested questions have reassured me that this has been a worthwhile project to pursue.

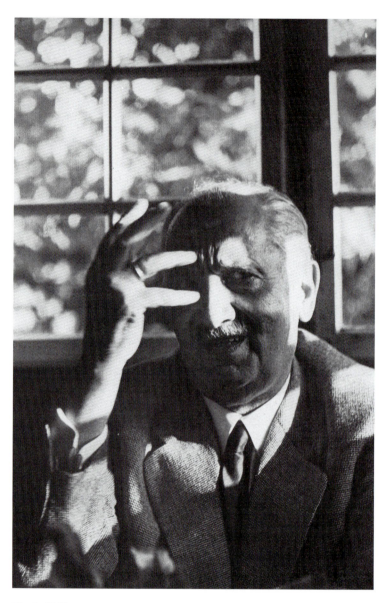

Martin Heidegger.

CHAPTER 1

Introduction

Few famous philosophers have written specifically for an audience of architects. Martin Heidegger is one of them. He spoke to a gathering of professionals and academics at a conference in Darmstadt in 1951. Hans Scharoun – later architect of the Berlin Philharmonie and German National Library – marked up his programme with glowing comments, enthusing about Heidegger's talk to friends and acquaintances (Blundell-Jones 1995, 136). The discussion, which so inspired Scharoun, was later printed as an essay called 'Building Dwelling Thinking'. Republished to this day and translated into many languages, the text influenced more than one generation of architects, theorists and historians during the latter half of the twentieth century. When Peter Zumthor waxes lyrical about the atmospheric potential of spaces and materials; when Christian Norberg-Schulz wrote about the spirit of place; when Juhani Pallasmaa writes about *The Eyes of the Skin*; when Dalibor Vesely argues about the crisis of representation; when Karsten Harries claims ethical parameters for architecture; when Steven Holl discusses phenomena and paints watercolours evoking architectural experiences; all these establishment figures are responding in some way to Heidegger and his notions of dwelling and place.

Not that the response to Heidegger has been overwhelmingly positive. Far from it. He remains perhaps the most controversial thinker among those who coloured the last deeply troubled century. Heidegger was a member of the Nazi party, triumphantly appointed rector of Freiburg University on the wave of terror and euphoria which brought the fascists to power in 1933. Whether the philosopher's resignation of that appointment the following year was the end of his infatuation, or whether he remained a lifelong Nazi, seems to depend as much on individual commentators' sympathy or antipathy for his philosophy as it does on the hotly contested facts of the case. Without doubt there are unpalatable moments in Heidegger's biography which should be acknowledged and condemned. However, when eminent architectural critics dismiss the philosopher in no uncertain terms – one has written an article titled 'Forget Heidegger' (after Jean Baudrillard's 'Forget Foucault') (Leach 2000) – they do so as much from the battleground of architecture's politics as they do from the moral high ground. Heidegger's reputation remains a matter of high stakes in the ivory towers of architectural academe. What is clear is that the philosopher resolutely romanticised the rural and the low-tech before, during and after Nazism, skating dangerously close to fascist rhetoric of 'blood and soil'. It also remains clear that a good deal of 'high' Western architecture – and architectural theory – from the latter half of the twentieth century owes a debt to Heidegger's influence.

Not that the response to Heidegger has been overwhelmingly positive. Far from it. He remains perhaps the most controversial thinker among those who coloured the last deeply troubled century.

What did this troubling philosopher say, then, about architecture? Why have so many architects listened? Heidegger challenged the procedures and protocols of professional practice, his standpoint on architecture part of a broader critique of the technocratic Western world. In a post-war era when Westerners seemed to justify their actions with increasing reference to economic and technical statistics, he pleaded that the immediacies of human experience shouldn't be forgotten. According to him, people make sense first through their inhabitation of their surroundings, and their emotional responses to them. Only then do they attempt to quantify their attitudes and actions through science and technology. Whereas others in the construction industry, like engineers and quantity surveyors, trade largely in data, the primary trade of architects is arguably in human experience. For the philosopher, building configures physically, over time, how people measure their place in the world. Indeed, by recording traces of human engagement physically at both large and small scales, buildings set out the particular ethos of every builder and dweller. In this way, architecture can help to centre people in the world. It can offer individuals places from which to inquire for themselves. Heidegger felt that this was how architecture had been understood in the past, and that the insatiable rise of technology had obscured that understanding.

Heidegger's model of architecture thus centred on qualities of human experience. His call to reintegrate building with dwelling – to reintegrate the making of somewhere with the activities and qualities of its inhabitation – celebrated non-expert architecture alongside the 'high' architecture of books and journals, finding architecture more at home with ongoing daily life than any sort of finished product. In the 1960s and 1970s, such thinking chimed with the work of architectural writers like Jane Jacobs (1961), Bernard Rudofsky (1964) and Christopher Alexander (1977a, 1977b) who also questioned the authority of professional expertise and sought instead to validate non-expert building. Architectural practitioners valued the challenges which Heidegger's work offered to the priorities of the industry in which they found themselves, and indeed to the priorities constituting Western society. Architectural academics, through Heidegger's writing, negotiated productive stories and images about activities of building, its origins and its representations.

Even in this short outline, distinctive characteristics of Heidegger's rhetoric emerge: a particular morality; a promotion of the value of human presence and inhabitation; an unapologetic mysticism; a tendency to nostalgia; and a drive to highlight the limits of science and technology. This rhetoric has its heroes and villains. The heroes are unaffected provincials, those somehow attuned to their bodies and emotions, and those prone to romanticise the past. The villains are statisticians and technocrats intent on mathematical quantification, professionals bent on appropriating everyday activities through legislative powers, and urban sophisticates in thrall to fashion. Dangers of the *milieu* of Heidegger's thinking are already apparent here. The potential for romantic myths of belonging to exclude people as well as include them, and a scepticism of high intellectual debate in favour of common sense, can veer toward totalitarianism. Unchecked, such thinking can lead in the direction of the fascist rhetoric with which Heidegger himself was involved, at least for a short time, in the 1930s.

Heidegger's work and controversy are seldom far apart. But no desire for controversy prompts what follows. This is an architect's book, written for architects by an architect. While it deals with philosophical writings, this book does not claim new philosophical insights or hope to solve philosophical questions. Rather, it aims to draw architects' attention to some of those questions, emphasising aspects of them which seem closest to the activities of a design studio. There are those for whom Heidegger's involvement with Nazism invalidates his work and, for them, this book is at best wasted effort and at worst complicity with a bad man and his troubling writing. I acknowledge this argument and sympathise with it. However it seems folly to pretend that Heidegger did not hold great influence over post-war expert architectural practice and thinking. He did – many influential practitioners and academics paid his work plenty of attention – and legacies of his influence persist. For that reason it's important to remember and appreciate the parameters of his arguments. My aim here is to help you approach the philosopher's texts for yourself. My advice, however, is caution. Keep up your critical guard. Where some architects have encountered productive design ideas and some scholars have found profound insights, others have encountered fundamental difficulties.

This book concentrates on Heidegger's 'Building Dwelling Thinking' – first published in 1951 – alongside two contemporary texts which help to amplify its ideas: 'The Thing' (1950); and '. . . poetically, Man dwells . . .' (1951). Some philosophers would find this focus puzzling. Throughout much of his life, Heidegger enjoyed the calculated display of anti-academic tendencies, inspired by devilment as much as conviction, frequently arguing for the instinctive over the learned dialogue of the academy (Safranski 1998, 128–129). Arguably, these essays of 1950–51 mark his furthest orbit from bookish philosophy, his most vehement rhetoric in favour of unmediated emotion. This is the period in Heidegger's work that philosophers cite least. However, although he wrote about architecture at other times in his life – notably in the 1935 text 'The Origin of the Work of Art' (translated 1971), as well as in *Being and Time* of 1927 (1962) and 'Art and Space' of 1971 (1973) – the three 1950–51 essays are arguably the most architectural of his writings precisely because it was here that he made amongst his most forthright claims for the authority of immediate experience.

Throughout much of his life, Heidegger enjoyed the calculated display of anti-academic tendencies, inspired by devilment as much as conviction, frequently arguing for the instinctive over the learned dialogue of the academy.

After this Introduction, the book begins with a mountain walk to introduce some of the philosopher's ideas, which are expanded and referenced in following sections. A short biography precedes a discussion of Heidegger's essays. My discussion is organised around the structure of each text with reference to other material where relevant. This approach maintains – for better or worse – some sense of the philosopher's rhetorical tactics and the circular mode of his arguments. It also allows you, should you wish, to follow Heidegger's texts alongside this book. All three essays are available in English translation in *Poetry, Language, Thought*, first published in 1971 and still in print, and references are given here to page numbers in that volume. The final section of this book explores how some architects and architectural commentators have interpreted Heidegger's thinking, organised around one particular example: Peter Zumthor's spa at Vals in Switzerland.

CHAPTER 2

A Mountain Walk

Heidegger stayed regularly at a hut built for him in 1922 above Todtnauberg in the Black Forest mountains, retreating there when he could. As he grew older, he philosophised about these circumstances: the forest walk became important to his writing and he gave at least one lecture on skiing. He claimed that thinking was analogous to following a forest path, naming one volume of essays *Holzwege* after forest paths, and another *Wegmarken*, waymarks, after the signs that help walkers stick to a trail. With this in mind, I invite you on a mountain walk to introduce some aspects of Heidegger's thinking concerning architecture, and some of its difficulties.

Although the philosopher's excursions followed paths in his beloved Black Forest, our walk will be in the English Lake District. We start at the small market town of Keswick which, in summer, does not have an air of calm. Its pavements, shops, pubs and tearooms swarm with tourists intent on an enjoyable day out: trippers arriving by coach, and families trying to forget their frustration at how long it took to park the car. Although the hills which surround the town and the adjacent lake of Derwentwater are a constant looming backdrop, their presence recedes behind frantic conviviality. As we head out of town towards the most brooding of the hills on the horizon, the grey mass of Skiddaw, the streets grow less busy, walking begins to calm us and a sense of mild relief takes hold. We turn from main road into side road, which becomes track and then path. Ten minutes later, the town already feels a world away. The next half hour is spent pre-occupied with climbing uphill, which is hard work, and the changing landscape gets little of our attention. But we must have become attuned to it because, when we reach the small overflowing car park at the base of the mountain proper, this tarmac outpost feels like an alien intrusion. We don't follow other walkers to the main hack up Skiddaw itself, but take a smaller path which curves up gently behind towards the base of a barren mountain valley. Here, we get our last glimpses for a while over Keswick, the car park and the walkers on their way to the peak. Alone now, we start to notice more. Our senses seem to have become more acute, or maybe we've just put aside some of our worries, because the birdsong and the adjacent stream seem louder, and shadows cast on the slopes by scudding clouds have caught our attention. We notice our own shadows projected onto the ground and grow more aware of the movement of our own bodies, and the stimulation of our senses.

Heidegger felt that aspects of everyday life, particularly in the Western world, served as distractions from the 'proper' priorities of human existence. For him, most of us, most of the time, were missing the point. He remained entranced by human 'being', by the question – which no parent can answer for their children – of why we are here or, in Leibniz's formulation which Heidegger liked, why there is not nothing. To him, the fact of human existence should not be routinely ignored but instead celebrated as central to life in all its richness and variation. Every human activity from the intellectual to the mundane, considered properly as he perceived it, derived authority from, and offered opportunities to explore philosophically, the ever central question of being. Yet, for Heidegger, most people immerse themselves in daily life in order to forget the big and difficult questions. The likes of worrying about parking the car in Keswick, or whether there will be a table in the tea room, were in the philosopher's view an all too comfortable distraction; a sort of occupational therapy allowing people to avoid confronting difficult questions about the raw fact of existence, and the implications of those questions.

Every human activity from the intellectual to the mundane, considered properly as he perceived it, derived authority from, and offered opportunities to explore philosophically, the ever central question of being.

To Heidegger, proper thinking was highly tuned to the fact of being and its traces. These traces, like our own shadow, the outline of the hills or the sounds of birdsong and stream, remain reminders of our miraculous presence. They're reminders of what a wonderful place the world can seem. To him, when we notice these reminders – when we remember to notice our own being – we achieve a kind of respite. Such moments, for Heidegger, allow people to locate themselves in a bigger picture, in a time span much longer than a life, and find an accommodating distance from petty concerns. The philosopher was prone to adorn his proper thinking with the rhetoric of rigour. He claimed that a disciplined openness was needed to hear and see in detail the veracity of the surrounding world. To think in this way was difficult work, seemingly best done alone. Heidegger was no enthusiast of Socratic dialogue, of the verbal sparring between scholars held up as a model of philosophy.

On our walk, we continue to climb slowly along the valley between the mountains of Skiddaw and Blencathra. The few scudding clouds gradually thicken into a blackening cloak covering the blue. No other soul is in sight, the only traces of movement the birds and a handful of sheep. The distant hills in front start to mist over. We realise that this mist is rain, and it's moving towards us along the valley. The peaks either side of us disappear. Up here, we can see weather moving around us and toward us. As the skies darken, this looks as though it might be a serious storm. We have time to put on our waterproof clothes. All of a sudden, we realise that the solitude of this walk is less benevolent than it first seemed. We're about to be a long way from home in a storm. As heavy rain begins, we hope that we won't lose our bearings.

Alongside Heidegger's yearning for rigour, he found being to resonate most loudly in contemporary life through moments of high emotion. Anyone who has been lost on a mountainside in mist or rain will appreciate the fear it can evoke. In the face of the elements, human powerlessness is focused sharply. Storms at sea, or earthquakes, or floods evoke similar feelings. To Heidegger, intensities of emotion, like falling in love or the death of someone close, also show how little control individuals have to wield. They indicate how close everyone remains to the immediacies of life and death, of being and nothing. For him, the props and preoccupations of daily life, the scientific and technological support systems over which we do have some control, are seldom of relevance or comfort in circumstances like these. Our being is thrust central to our attention, whether we like it or not, and our favourite distractions are relegated. For Heidegger, being and its alternative should continue to inspire awe among us. According to his thinking, we lose our bearings when we forget the continued presence and potential might of being.

To Heidegger, intensities of emotion, like falling in love or the death of someone close, also show how little control individuals have to wield.

Although it's scary when the rain envelops us, bouncing off the ground and soaking our waterproofs, the storm isn't what we feared. It passes quickly, the skies clear and we breathe a sigh of relief. As we walk, the peaks reappear, the valley widens and a distant house surrounded by a handful of windblown trees heaves into view. The long low building with its steeply pitched roof nestles into a south-facing bank with an external terrace levelled in front. The familiar scale of its windows and doors, lined up in two rows, are hugely dominated by the surrounding peaks. As we approach, it becomes obvious that the stone walls are built from the rock of the hills themselves. There is clearly no road to this house, nor any connections to mains services. It's the only sign of human inhabitation in this valley, a long way from the nearest neighbour and quite a climb above it. Closer still, it becomes apparent that the structure – which a sign tells us was until recently Skiddaw House Youth Hostel – is now closed up and neglected.

For Heidegger, just as the authority of being overshadowed everyday life, it also overshadowed building. To him, building located human existence. He believed that building was set out around human presence, configured by it but also configuring the activities of that presence over time. At best, a structure was built by its inhabitants according to their needs and then configured and reconfigured through the ways in which they dwelt. The inhabitants' lives, in turn, were configured by the building. To him, the very fact of a building also stood for human presence. For Heidegger, a building was built according to the specifics of place and inhabitants, shaped by its physical and human topography. It was also built from fruits of the earth: stone; timber; and metals. For Heidegger, building was less about abstract objects than located individuals. And the form of a building could report the ethos of those individuals. Its details could be read for their aspirations and ideals. Moreover, the figure of a building dealt in presences and absences; as well as demonstrating the presence of an inhabitant, it could also show their absence.

For Heidegger, a building was built according to the specifics of place and inhabitants, shaped by its physical and human topography.

Considered according to Heidegger's way of thinking, Skiddaw House Hostel located human life in the valley, standing for human presence there. It was built according to the needs of its first inhabitants. The building then shaped their lives, and they continued to shape the building through their daily occupation of it. Its materials were largely quarried and harvested in the vicinity, probably within sight of the building. Construction was determined to some extent by the materials available. The building was also adapted to the local microclimate: buried into the bank to maximise exposure to the southern sun and to shelter against the cold north. Its pitched roof derived from the practicalities of shedding rain and snow at a spot so exposed. Its unadorned fenestration derived from the light and ventilation needs of the rooms behind. Built thus, Skiddaw House can be interpreted as reporting of a way of understanding the world around, related to people and the places and materials they found to hand, of which Heidegger would sympathise. But the building's adaptation into a youth hostel and its subsequent closure also speak of the passing of that way of life, and that way of understanding, in this place. The house cannot be maintained. No longer do people want to live there, nor do enough people enjoy staying somewhere so remote from the comforts of Western life. The upkeep of Skiddaw House has become too expensive. At once, the building stands for the sometime presence of an ethos not dissimilar to that advocated by Heidegger, and also for its contemporary absence. Semi-derelict, the house is a conspicuous fragment of the past.

We retrace our steps with the thought of taking another path back: one which branches off to the opposite side of the valley. The grass is long here and it's rocky underfoot, demanding constant attention, so we find it difficult to watch for this new path. Sheep have also made a number of trails, and we have to keep stopping to see whether these are what we're looking for. We must have taken one of these sheep trails accidentally, because it peters out, and we have to return to the track where we began. Only when the second track reaches a plank deliberately placed over a stream do we know we're on the right path.

Around the time that Heidegger wrote the three essays concerning architecture outlined in this book, he suggested that thinking was rather like following a *Holzweg*, a woodman's path in the Black Forest. He made much of this analogy. Woodman's paths were disorienting, surrounded by a dense matrix of tree trunks, and few distant views were possible. To the philosopher, a walker follows a path in faith that it must lead somewhere. But when walking, or thinking, it often remains difficult to be sure one is on the right track. And the path might lead to a dead end, or lead round in a circle. Only occasional arrival at a clearing, which may be familiar or allow a view out over the wider landscape, has potential to prove orientation for sure. Thinking, to Heidegger, involved following a path that has been more or less inscribed in the ground by others who have been there before, following the most promising turns, occasionally getting lost and occasionally arriving at the light and comparative orientation of a forest clearing. Thinking, in this model, involves wandering from a starting point and remaining open to findings reached on the way. It involves no organised system or logical process. According to Heidegger, any attempt to systemise thinking – to abstract it as logic or quantify it as a process – was a flawed reduction. Thinking involved rushes of inspiration with potential to surprise the thinker. It occurred in moments of clarity as a gift to be received, its origins remaining ultimately mysterious. For Heidegger, being – the first direction of thought – could not be readily summarised or contained by a system. Heidegger's was a reverential, mystical model of thinking which sought to promote the authority of being, as he understood it, and counter the systemising impulse that he associated with false certainties erected by science and technology. Instead, for him, the authority of thinking derived from the value of each person's distinctive judgement.

Thinking, to Heidegger, involved following a path that has been more or less inscribed in the ground by others who have been there before, following the most promising turns, occasionally getting lost and occasionally arriving at the light and comparative orientation of a forest clearing.

Signs of everyday life become visible again as our path descends out of the valley. First, we see other walkers descending Skiddaw. Then houses come into view on the hillside opposite and finally we see the main road some distance below us. We turn towards it, down towards the river and a path that will take us back into Keswick, to the promise of a drink and a wholesome meal.

Heidegger wrote of the mountain life from which he drew philosophical influence as 'up there', referring to moral authority as well as to altitude. In attributing such authority to the raw presences and natural rhythms of the mountains, in particular to what he perceived as their privileged access to being, the philosopher emphasised the increasing absence of the lessons he found in such landscapes from many lives in the Western world. Moments of awareness of our own presence, often brought home to us by our senses, emotions and the phenomena of nature, had become rare opportunities to him. He felt that we were losing the ability to appreciate our existence in the context of a sweep far longer and broader than our own lives. Heidegger's attribution of special authority to these landscapes of being, as he perceived them, is marked by his tendency to romanticism.

The English Lake District, the site of our walk, epitomises romanticism. It has been admired by famous romantics including the metaphysical poet William Wordsworth and landscape painter J.M.W. Turner. As a tendency, romanticism is characterised by introspection, emotion and sensitivity: an awe at natural forces and a perceived transcendence of nature over human affairs. Such qualities infuse Heidegger's work on dwelling and place. Romanticism has its critics, who accuse it of naive optimism and an abdication of responsibility. To them, the romantic can be so entranced by solitary poetising that she or he fails to perceive human evils and hardships around them. In a British context – due in part to the legacy of Wordsworth and Turner, as well as John Ruskin and the two Williams, Blake and Morris – romanticism has overtones of innocence. It has been the province of obscure dreamers, manifested in outdoor pursuits rendered institutional by the Boy Scouts, the Rambler's Association and Youth Hostels Association. But romanticism in a German context is far more difficult. Nazism was larded with invocations which can be linked to the romantic, such as *'Blut und Boden'* ('blood and soil'). And the heroes of German romanticism loom large in Heidegger's writings before, during and after the Nazi ascendancy. Many see Heidegger's penchant for romanticism as one of the most dangerous aspects of his philosophy. Where there are those who honour their locality and celebrate a sense of belonging, others can be cast out as not belonging. And here are the seeds of racism and persecution. When the romantic reifies the land, ugly things might be done in the name of that land.

But romanticism in a German context is far more difficult. Nazism was larded with invocations which can be linked to the romantic, such as 'Blut und Boden' ('blood and soil').

Heidegger was scathing of tourists, who he felt visited but did not see. Surrounded by the landscape only fleetingly, they were unable to perceive the vital traces of being which the philosopher found there. Heidegger vehemently held certain ways of life to be authentic and others to be inauthentic. For many critics, led by Theodor Adorno whose commentary will be discussed below, these authenticity claims are among the most challenging aspects of Heidegger's work. Such claims admit two sorts: the knowing *cognoscenti*, Heideggerians who appreciate clues of being; and those who do not know, or have not been taught, how to see. For Adorno and others, authenticity is dangerous because it is divisive and potentially exclusive – particularly where appropriated as culturally specific; in this case as distinctively German. Here again is the germ of racism.

Whether this mountain walk leaves you as a tourist or a Heideggerian, as a subscriber to the authenticity of mountain landscape or a critic, it has introduced a number of notions which will be developed throughout this book; notions: of being; of building and dwelling; of science and technology; of system and mysticism; of presences and absences; of authenticity and exclusion. These themes pervade 'The Thing', 'Building Dwelling Thinking' and '. . . poetically, Man dwells . . .'. But one more diversion is necessary before we encounter these texts.

CHAPTER 3

Placing Heidegger

Heidegger's life can be characterised by the places where he lived and wrote. The philosopher's youth was centred on a small town in provincial Southern Germany, Messkirch, where he was born in 1889. Heidegger's father was sexton to the town's church. This role determined much about the family's life and, in 1895, they moved into a tied house associated with it (Safranski 1997, 1–16). The house, along with the church and the town square in-between, became young Heidegger's playground [see below]. Enlisted as a chorister and bell-ringer, his life was organised by the clock and the calendar of Catholicism. The church also funded Heidegger's education with a series of scholarships. He was sent to boarding schools, first in Konstanz and then in Freiburg-im-Breisgau, with the aim of training for the priesthood. Heidegger began wrestling with theological and philosophical questions at a young age; both at school and on

Heidegger's childhood playground, the church square in Messkirch, with his parents' former house to the left and the church to the right.

A track near Messkirch where Heidegger claimed to have begun wrestling with philosophical ideas as a youth, looking back over the town.

long country walks during vacations back in Messkirch (Heidegger 1981b) [see above]. It is perhaps no surprise that he later advocated a similarly tight ordering of location, routine and ethos when he wrote about dwelling and place; and that he continued to find prompts to thinking in the movements of nature.

Heidegger entered a Jesuit institution briefly at the age of seventeen but it didn't suit him. Instead he turned to the academic study of theology and philosophy at The Albert Ludwig University of Freiburg. In 1907, Messkirch's parish priest gave Heidegger a philosophy book by Franz Brentano titled *On the Manifold Meaning of Being According to Aristotle*, which shaped his lifelong interest in the theme of being (Ott 1993, 51). Through Brentano, who taught Edmund Husserl, Heidegger became attracted to Husserl's book *Logical Investigations*. Following Heidegger's teaching qualification thesis of 1915, concerning the mystic theologian Duns Scotus, Husserl became professor of philosophy in Freiburg and the two men became acquainted.

Heidegger married Elfride Petri in 1917, a Lutheran Protestant from Prussia. By then he was working as a teaching assistant at the university in Freiburg, soon to become Husserl's assistant. Theodor Kisiel, in his book *The Genesis of Heidegger's Being and Time* suggests that Heidegger was now beginning to forge a distinctive philosophical position from his readings of, among others, Husserl, Aristotle, Augustine, Dilthey, Kant, Kierkegaard and Luther (1993, 452–458). These studies set him on a path which led him to reject the philosophy of religion and the practice of Catholicism, breaking from his oldest friends and the belief system which had ordered his childhood. This decision may have related to the end of his dependence on church grants and the Protestant background of his new wife, and also perhaps to his aspiration to join the primarily Protestant academic elite (Ott 1993, 106–121).

With the support of Husserl, now Heidegger's friend and mentor, the young philosopher was appointed professor at Marburg University from 1923. He and his family (two sons were born in 1918 and 1920) moved to that city but disliked it. They travelled whenever possible to a mountain hut built for them a few months before at Todtnauberg, approximately 20 kilometres from Freiburg [see below]. Heidegger attributed providential authority to this small building and its landscape, which figured increasingly large in his life and thought over the next fifty years (Sharr 2006). He spoke in 1934 about how philosophy found him there as a susceptible scribe, almost suspending the landscape in words through him without his involvement (Heidegger 1981a). In the mountains, Heidegger established an intense routine of living, writing, chopping wood, eating, sleeping, walking and skiing: a way of life which became as concentrated and ordered as his childhood in Messkirch.

Physically short, speaking with a strong regional accent and dressing almost like a farmer, his remarkably intense lecturing style bewitched many in his audience.

Although he disliked Marburg and its academic community, Heidegger cut a distinctive figure there as a young professor (Löwith 1994, 29–30; Gadamer 1994, 114–116). Physically short, speaking with a strong regional accent and dressing almost like a farmer, his remarkably intense lecturing style bewitched

Heidegger's mountain hut at Todtnauberg, which was central to his life and thought.

many in his audience. His circular manner of questioning, loaded with rhetorical questions, had great effect. Heidegger's reputation spread like wildfire among students, a surprisingly large number of whom later made philosophical careers for themselves, including Hannah Arendt, famed for her political philosophy (and whose love affair with the philosopher is now much discussed), Hans-Georg Gadamer, famed for his work on hermeneutics, and Herbert Marcuse, famed for his Marxist philosophy (Wolin 2001).

Heidegger returned to Freiburg from Marburg in 1928 to take up one of Germany's most celebrated professorships in philosophy there, succeeding Husserl on his retirement. This post was secured following the impact of Heidegger's book *Being and Time*, still his most famous text, published in incomplete form the previous year. Although a suburban house was built for the philosopher and his family at Zähringen on the outskirts of the city, he continued to retreat to the Todtnauberg hut when he could.

Largely due to the international reception of *Being and Time*, Heidegger was something of a public intellectual by the early 1930s. When the Nazis seized power in April 1933, he became rector of Freiburg University amid frenzied political restructuring. Almost simultaneously he joined the Nazi party, to a timetable scheduled to maximise publicity, and helped to implement some of their academic policies. He gave speeches in which he mixed his distinctive philosophical vocabulary with fascist propaganda (Heidegger 1992). The philosopher resigned his rectorship in April 1934, reputedly disillusioned with the regime, returning to research and teaching. Heidegger claimed that his ambitions for the university – seemingly to reorganise it according to his own philosophy – had been thwarted. However, he implemented a number of Nazi policies during his time in office including directives on 'race' affecting Jewish academics, whose number included Husserl. According to Heidegger's contested post-war apologia (1985), he spent the remaining Hitler years in quiet resistance of the regime. He studied Friedrich Nietzsche's philosophy and the writings of poet Friedrich Hölderlin, both of whom figured in Nazi rhetoric. In 1946, the university declared him to have put his reputation at the service of the regime and his teaching was judged too 'unfree' for contemporary circumstances (Ott 1993, 309–351). As a result, the philosopher was forcibly retired, pensioned and prevented from teaching until further notice.

Commentators write of a 'turn' in Heidegger's work at some point between the early 1930s and 1950 (Hoy 1993). The timing of this turn appears to be as much a matter of the critic's sympathy or antipathy for Heidegger as of philosophical merit, because it is assumed to coincide with his disillusionment with Nazism. The philosopher's later work drew from those he felt thought from first principles. He studied mystic theologians anew and became increasingly concerned with the philosophical potential of German poetry, particularly that of Hölderlin, Rilke and Trakl. He also looked to the earliest philosophers, the pre-Socratics (of whose texts only enigmatic fragments remain) and more covertly to sources from the Eastern tradition (May 1996)

The university senate relaxed Heidegger's teaching ban in 1950 following petitions from his sympathisers. He was granted the status of emeritus professor in 1951 and his teaching suspension was formally lifted (Ott 1993, 309–371).

The philosopher subsequently wrote and gave occasional lectures, continuing to spend time at his mountain hut. He worked into his final years, visiting Messkirch regularly and sometimes attending services in the church there, taking his old seat in the choir stalls.

The philosopher died on 26 May 1976 in Freiburg. He was buried, at his request, in the graveyard belonging to the church at Messkirch. The philosopher asked for a star to be carved on top of his headstone, rather than the cross which adorns surrounding graves, echoing the carved star on top of the well adjacent to his Todtnauberg hut. Buried with him were branches from the Black Forest and the wind chime that hung outside his hut's study window. These final requests seem to demonstrate Heidegger's accommodation, rather than reconciliation, with the order of his childhood, affirming a commitment to the philosophy he found in the order of his mountain life.

Near the end of his life, at a seminar in Le Thor in 1969, Heidegger claimed that the path of his thought had three stages: first, his work up to *Being and Time*; second, the period between that book and his turn; and third, the period after that turn. Each of these, he suggested, could be characterised by one of three words: consecutively 'Meaning – Truth – Place' (Casey 1997, 279). Less concerned with participating in philosophical dialectic, instead trying to forge an unfamiliar vocabulary from old meanings of familiar words, Heidegger's writings from this third stage often seem strange and idiosyncratic. It is significant for architects that Heidegger chose to summarise these writings with the term 'place'. He referred not only to the sites where he himself thought, particularly his mountain hut, but also to the significance of thought placed in particular contexts, a many-sided notion expanded in the three texts which will now be considered.

CHAPTER 4

Heidegger's Thinking on Architecture

Heidegger's three key essays concerning architecture, 'The Thing' (1950), 'Building Dwelling Thinking' (1951), and '. . . poetically, Man dwells . . .' (1951), were written when Germany was undergoing massive political and social rebuilding following World War Two. Western allies established the Federal Republic of Germany (West Germany) in 1949 and the partition of the German Democratic Republic (East Germany), a separate state with a competing ideology, was also realised. The raw business of survival had been immediate for vast numbers of hungry and displaced people at the end of the war and was not far from most minds. Destruction had been widespread and physical rebuilding was still in its infancy. One-fifth of all German homes were destroyed between 1939 and 1945. Post-war estimates suggested that, in West Germany – where Heidegger's Freiburg and Black Forest were located – two-and-a-half million houses were required for refugees from the East, along with another million for a generation of younger families (Conrads 1962). In Heidegger's Freiburg, as elsewhere, families and friends shared accommodation until they could find a flat or house of their own. The term *Wohnungsfrage*, literally 'dwelling question', was coined to describe this housing crisis which lasted well into the 1950s. Heidegger's discussion of dwelling in 'Building Dwelling Thinking' and its companion texts was in direct response to this question.

The dwelling question wasn't just of general interest to Heidegger; it was also a personal concern. Many associated the philosopher with the Nazi regime in the immediate aftermath of war, including occupying forces in Freiburg and his fellow academics. Just as bombed-out civilians were in dire need of accommodation in 1945, so were the occupying powers, and a programme was begun to requisition houses of Nazi sympathisers. Under this programme, Heidegger's house in the Freiburg suburbs was declared a 'party residence'. As a result, the philosopher and his family were compelled to share their house with one or two further families for 'some years' (Ott 1993, 312). When Heidegger wrote about the question of dwelling, he did so with personal experience of the requisitioning of his house.

At around the same time, Freiburg University called de-Nazification hearings to begin reorganising the institution and Heidegger was summoned to account for himself. The tribunal had the power not only to fire academics but to seize their books in order to restock the damaged university library; both a necessity and a public humiliation. Heidegger was not subject to this punishment, although it seemed likely for a while. Instead he was declared unfit for teaching and retired on full pension (Ott 1993, 307–351). This decision was revisited in 1950 and his permission to teach was reinstated. The invitation to present 'The Thing' in June that year was the philosopher's first public appearance following his rehabilitation. 'Building Dwelling Thinking', presented to the conference on 'Man and Space' in August 1951, and '. . . poetically, Man dwells . . .' delivered at the fashionable Bühler Höhe spa in Baden Baden, were among the philosopher's next appearances. The papers explored here thus remain significant within the context of Heidegger's work not just because they address issues of the time, but also because they were among the philosopher's first lectures after his imposed silence.

The papers explored here thus remain significant within the context of Heidegger's work not just because they address issues of the time, but also because they were among the philosopher's first lectures after his imposed silence.

Perhaps because Heidegger addressed them to public audiences, the three texts are as polemical as they are philosophical. They approach related questions in similar ways. Each text amplifies the thinking of the others. In all three, he chose to explore an aspect of contemporary existence that indicated an unfavourable comparison with the past as he saw it, offering a tragic view of contemporary human experience which he sought to mitigate.

Heidegger found etymology, the history of the meanings of words, to be a source of insight. He worked as an etymological archaeologist; mining meanings of familiar words and using what he found to question received understanding. Heidegger felt that he was breaking open familiar contemporary language to find the old (and thus for him the authentic) meanings hidden there. George Steiner suggests that:

> Heidegger is carrying to violent extremes the hermenuetic paradox whereby the interpreter knows better than the author, whereby interpretation, where it is inspired and probing enough can 'go behind' the visible text to the hidden roots of its inception and meaning. This, undoubtedly, is how Heidegger operates, and on the level of normal expository responsibility, many of his readings are opportunistic fictions. (1992: 143)

In each of the papers considered here, Heidegger derived from the archaic meaning of particular words the same interpretation of the preconditions of existence, which recur in support of his thinking on architecture and his distinctive model of how people make sense of the world.

'The Thing'

'*Das Ding*', 'The Thing', was an invited lecture presented to the Bavarian Academy of Fine Arts in Munich on 6 June 1950. Heidegger's audience – consisting of academy members, academics and students – overfilled the lecture theatre, spilling into aisles and gangways. The paper was published in the academy's yearbook of 1951 and subsequently in the 1954 volume *Vorträge und Aufsätze* (*Lectures and Writings*).

'The Thing' was written as a philosophical investigation of life's paraphernalia, which Heidegger termed 'things'. The key themes of the text are decisive to Heidegger's view of architecture, not least because he discussed buildings in 'Building Dwelling Thinking' as 'built things' (1971, 152). The essay 'The Thing' is dense, complex and proceeds in Heidegger's characteristic circular fashion. The philosopher argued that distances were shrinking in the post-war world because of international travel and mass media. He claimed that this had negative consequences; particularly that humans' proximity to their own existence was diminishing. Heidegger linked this notion of 'nearness' to a notion of 'thingness' by suggesting how a thing related to the preconditions of its own existence. Naming those preconditions 'the fourfold', he argued that any thing 'gathers' this fourfold, helping individuals become closer to the world around them (complex notions that will be considered in detail below). Heidegger considered each of these terms carefully and shaped his argument from their definition. Underpinning the paper was a judgement that science and technology remained inadequate to help individuals make sense of their daily experiences. These themes – concerning firstly individuals' sense of proximity and its influence on their engagement with the world around them, secondly how people conceive of the things around them, and thirdly how they relate to the basic constituents of the world – are revisited with specific regard to architecture in 'Building Dwelling Thinking'.

This is perhaps the point of the text and its companions: to confront the reader with another view of the world.

On first reading, 'The Thing' can seem very strange indeed to someone with a modern scientific Western education. The philosopher seems to cast himself as the reader's philosophical guide and spiritual mentor, a self-appointed secular preacher. His writings have mystical dimensions which fit uncomfortably with the scientific priorities of conventional education. This is perhaps the point of the text and its companions: to confront the reader with another view of the world. 'The Thing' is amongst Heidegger's most challenging texts because of its palpable difference. Like much of his work, it must be indulged if it is to be explored.

Nearness

Heidegger began 'The Thing' by discussing changes to perceptions of distance in modern life. He attributed these to faster travel and to mass media: radio, film and television. He felt that popular understandings of 'nearness' and 'remoteness' had changed and implied that this change was negative. To discuss this situation, Heidegger posed the question: 'What about nearness? How can we come to know its nature?' (1971, 166). Heidegger responded to his own question with a further question:

> **Nearness, it seems, cannot be encountered directly. We succeed in reaching it rather than by attending to what is near. Near to us are what we call things. But what is a thing? Man has so far given no more thought to the thing as a thing than he has to nearness. (1971: 166)**

This quotation employs rhetorical tactics which recur throughout Heidegger's writings: he sought to cloak familiar language and familiar ideas in a cloud of mystery. He wanted to make the notion of 'nearness' more problematic, crowding-in on one another the word's separate but associated connotations of familiarity, intellectual proximity and physical proximity. In doing so, he set out to redefine nearness according to his own priorities. He began by linking individuals' appreciation of nearness with their relationship to 'things' and attempting to imbue the question with a sense of radical simplicity.

Heidegger introduced a physical example in order to discuss things. He wrote about a hypothetical jug ('*der Krug*') to explore how people might understand being near to a thing. The particular choice of example was crucial to the development of his argument, and appears related to a verse of the *Tao Te Ching* which discusses a jug. 'The *Tao*' by Lao Tse, a mystical thinker who lived in the Hunan province of China probably in the sixth century BCE, is a key work in Eastern philosophy, some of whose verses Heidegger attempted to translate to German in 1946 (May 1996, 6–7). Heidegger may also have had in mind Aristotle's *Physics*, in which place is considered as a receptacle (Aristotle 1983, 28–29; Casey 1997, 50–71).

For Heidegger, the jug is its own thing, 'self-supporting ['*Selbständiges*'] [. . .] independent' (1971, 167). Heidegger asserted that, by virtue of this: 'When we take the jug as a made vessel, then surely we are apprehending it – so it seems – as a thing and never a mere object'. Just over two pages into 'The Thing', we are already in deep. This somewhat coy statement, in Heideggerian code, contains at least two major challenges to the way of thinking prevalent in Western society. It's important to listen carefully to Heidegger's turns of phrase. First that 'so it seems', almost casually arranged between parentheses, is a rallying call. It seeks to validate the authority of immediate human experience over abstract philosophical truths. It contains the suggestion that the world is first and foremost perceived by how it seems to each thinking individual. Second, Heidegger poses a distinction between 'thing' and 'object'. This is a decisive manoeuvre. It challenges what Heidegger felt was a prevailing Western outlook: that the ephemera around us comprises objects. It's important to consider both these challenges here because they introduce key aspects of what the philosopher has to say about architecture. Both the notion that the world is appreciated according to how it seems to you and me as thinking individuals, and the relationship of thing to object, need to be considered before we can proceed with Heidegger's discussion of his hypothetical jug.

So it seems

A sense of the tangible presence of existence pervades 'The Thing' and Heidegger's writings about dwelling and place. Most commentators agree that Heidegger's lifelong philosophical pursuit was directed toward being. The title of his first major work, *Being and Time* (1962) indicates that emphasis and the quotation he chose to begin the book, from the Eleatic Stranger in Plato's *Sophist*, arguably summarises its project:

> **For manifestly you have long been aware of what you mean when you use the expression '*being*'. We, however, who used to think that we understood it, have now become perplexed. (1962: 1)**

This quotation, which again seeks to mystify the familiar, offers a statement of purpose: Heidegger introduced being as a primary concern and questioned its received understanding. The philosopher's explorations of dwelling and place can be considered as one of many routes that he tried to follow in trying to make sense of the question of being; exploring the situation of being in the physical world of things.

Heidegger's interpretation of being began with the simple fact that humans are. To him, this was the first question of philosophy. Basic and fundamental, it was a question he felt most philosophers ignored or forgot. In this, Heidegger followed phenomenology, a strand of thought shaped by Edmund Husserl, who himself responded to thinkers including Hegel and Schopenhauer. Such phenomenology begins with the bare fact of human existence, arguing that the world is always already there before anyone tries to reflect upon it. It proposes that immediate contact with existence has become clouded in contemporary society, that people should attempt to re-establish contact with it, and that it has philosophical status. For Heidegger, being was primarily phenomenological rather than cerebral: he believed that it was largely pre-intellectual, and that thinking about being was a subsequent activity. Rüdiger Safranski calls this, in his biography of Heidegger, studying the laws of free fall whilst falling (1998, 115); which is to say that individuals are always already alive before trying to think about life. In the philosopher's scheme, each of us exists before we start thinking, and before we start trying to think about our own existence.

Heidegger's interpretation of being began with the simple fact that humans are. To him, this was the first question of philosophy.

This was a radical position because it challenged the prevailing philosophical conception of the world, or at least that prevailing among Anglo-American philosophers. Put simply, it might be said that such philosophers, after Aristotle, perceive the world more or less as a 'primacy of substances' (Frede 1993, 45). Thought was separate from the world in a system in which an observer categorises the world around them from a position of intellectual detachment. Heidegger was uneasy with this detached notion of thinking, which for him directed the impetus of philosophy away from daily immediacies of being. To him, it was only possible to begin trying to understand the world from a starting point already enmeshed in the familiar everyday language, priorities and things of the world. Heidegger's distinctive argument was that philosophical pursuit of being inevitably started from the condition of being. He established his notion of being in relation to its alternative, nothing. If existence was the first question of philosophy, then it was fundamentally highlighted by the possibility of its opposite: non-existence. He referred to human presence and absence, to life and death. For Heidegger, philosophy began with the remarkable but often overlooked fact that human life exists.

Heidegger pursued his argument about the hypothetical jug in 'The Thing' by linking these notions of presence and absence. The philosopher argued that the jug's use consisted in its void: although the jug is a recognisable something in its physicality, it is the void of the jug – the nothing at its core – that makes the thing useful. The philosopher here seems to refer to verse 11 of the *Tao Te Ching*: 'One hollows the clay and shapes it into pots:/ In their nothingness consists the pot's effectiveness' (Tse 1989, 31). Heidegger set up this understanding of a jug in opposition to what he considered its scientific interpretation as received through more orthodox philosophy. He suggested that a jug could never be empty in science, its contents merely one fluid, air, displaced by another, wine. Heidegger questioned whether this model corresponded with how people relate to using a jug. Do people primarily understand the filling and pouring of a jug like this? He felt it significant that science had no means to consider emptiness. Science's inability to measure nothingness – either as what makes a jug useful or as the all-important opposite of being – exemplified for him the broader inadequacy of scientific methods for describing human experience.

When Heidegger wrote about his hypothetical jug in 'The Thing' that 'we are apprehending it – so it seems – as a thing and never a mere object', his caveat 'so it seems' sought to emphasise that any appreciation of the jug should belong with being. The world, and the jug, should be understood primarily through how they seem to us as individuals through our own experience; less according to abstract categories. The jug is immediate and real. The individual grasps it physically, picks it up, understands it manually because of its tangible characteristics, because of what it feels like. Thinking about this thing only properly begins *after* the physical presence of the thinker and the presence of the jug, together. Although this may seem at first a nit-picking distinction, it comes to have much broader implications for Heidegger's philosophical scheme and his thinking on architecture.

Thing and object

When Heidegger argued that the jug should be apprehended 'as a thing and never a mere object', he promoted his notion of the thing as something more than an object. He advocated an alternative to the idea of object prevailing in Anglo-American philosophy where the individual is promoted as a detached observer. The thinking of this detached observer aspires to a higher plane, distinct from the day to day messiness of existence; where forms, pure ideas, each an original model or archetype, are addressed by the mind. Sensible things, ordinary things, are derived from these forms as lesser copies. A tree, for example, exists as a pure idea on a higher plane and also in reproduction in the real trees that accompany everyday life. These pure forms of each object were considered in relation to the singular form of beauty. They were transcendent; which is to say that they were perceived as remaining timeless, truthful and authoritative.

For Heidegger, conceiving of things as objects once again diminished the importance of being. To distinguish between the things of everyday life and some notional transcendent object-form was to set up an unhelpful distraction from immediate experience. To him, things are appreciated primarily through their engagement in everyday human life. Heidegger suggested in 'The Thing' that a potter made the jug as a self-supporting thing for the particular purpose of holding liquid. He acknowledged that the jug had an appearance – its Platonic 'eidos' or 'idea' which he defined as 'what stands forth' – deriving both from how it was made and from its perception when a human considers it (1971, 168). However, Heidegger argued, the jug is distinguished as a thing primarily because humans have a physical and intellectual relationship with it. He suggested in 'The Thing': 'That is why Plato, who conceives of the presence of what is present in terms of the outward appearance, had no more understanding of the nature of the thing than did Aristotle and all subsequent thinkers' (1971, 168). For Heidegger, the purity, beauty and timelessness of the visual idea remained secondary, far removed from daily practicalities of use.

To him, it was the practicalities of everyday life which first bring humans into contact – physical and intellectual – with the paraphernalia of life.

Heidegger found the notion of object inadequate: too abstract, too pretentious, too detached from daily experience. In contrast, a thing, for him, gained its characteristics from use: what it was like to hold; and how it related humans to the world around them. A thing was part of human being, not an abstract realm, always already there before people tried to think about it.

. . . it was the practicalities of everyday life which first bring humans into contact – physical and intellectual – with the paraphernalia of life.

Fourfold: the preconditions of existence

Having opposed his notion of thing to that of object and promoted the validity of experience over scientific reduction, Heidegger's argument in 'The Thing', already idiosyncratic to the uninitiated, next takes an even more curious turn. He sought to set out the basic conditions of existence in which humans experience things, naming it 'the fourfold'. These conditions are revisited in 'Building Dwelling Thinking' as the conditions in which people experience buildings. The specific example of the jug remained important to his case.

Returning to the void at the centre of the jug, Heidegger argued that the jug's empty state, suggesting its ability to pour, was the decisive aspect of its character. Although many such 'outpourings' were simply drinks for people, the philosopher was particularly interested in the sacred potential of the jug's 'poured gift' ('*das Geschenk*', literally a present). A jug could pour water and wine in regular circumstances, but it could also pour for consecration. He likened this special pouring, from the nothing at the core of the jug, to a natural spring whose supply seemed to have a mysterious provenance. His thinking here may have related to the spring outside the study window of his mountain hut at Todtnauberg, to whose life-giving water supply he accorded reverential status (Sharr 2006, 73). He suggested that the jug, like such a source, sustains:

> the marriage of '*Erde*' ['earth'] and '*Himmel*' ['sky', but also 'heaven' in German] [. . .] the wine given by the fruit of the vine, the fruit in which the earth's nourishment and the sky's sun are betrothed to one another. (1971: 180)

For Heidegger it was important that the jug, made from earth, connected human experience of earth and sky. He developed this connection by analysing his notion of poured gift, considering in support the etymology of the German root '*Guß*' which is similar to the English 'gush'. The German carries additional meanings to the English: the expression '*aus einem Guß*' refers to formulating a unified whole; '*das Gießen*' is a casting; '*Guß-beton*' is cast concrete and '*Guß-eisen*' cast iron. Such connotations are vital to Heidegger's point here, which is that the jug and its drink – linked to sky through the etymology of '*Geschenk*' – is a unified whole, a little casting of heaven. When the jug poured, for the philosopher, it gave for humans a drop of the mysterious source of life. He attributed sacred qualities to the jug's ability to give.

Heidegger developed his suggestion that the jug might have sacred resonance. To him, the jug united earth and sky because its poured gift could indicate to mortals ('*Sterblichen*', related to '*sterben*', to die) something of their life with divinities ('*Göttlichen*', gods, related to '*göttlich*', divine). He suggested that: 'In the gift of outpouring, mortals and divinities each dwell in their different ways' (1971, 173). Heidegger didn't offer a definition of any of these terms, inferring that earth, sky, divinities and mortals derived authority from mutual definition. He suggested that the four remain conjoined in 'mirror-play' ('*Spiegel-spiel*'), an inevitable reflection of one another that was the primary pre-condition of existence. Heidegger felt that in earth, sky, divinities and mortals together consisted the primary circumstance of existence, naming this circumstance 'the fourfold' ('*das Geviert*').

Heidegger suggested that:

> In the gift of outpouring that is the drink, mortals stay in their own way.
> In the gift of outpouring that is a libation, the divinities stay in their own
> way [. . .] In the gift of outpouring, mortals and divinities each dwell in
> their different ways. Earth and sky dwell in the gift of the outpouring. In
> the gift of the outpouring earth and sky, mortals and divinities each dwell in
> their different ways [. . .] These four, at one because of what they themselves
> are, belong together. Preceding everything that is present, they are enfolded
> into a single fourfold. (1971: 173)

The philosopher wrote of 'staying' and 'dwelling'. Earth, sky, divinities and other
mortals, to him, presented timeless opportunities for us to orientate ourselves.
The four are always together, around us, and as such provide a single reference
point. Because we are always already in alignment with them, they offer us
opportunities to appreciate our own qualities and characteristics. Commonalities
and differences are made apparent by reference to constituents of the fourfold.
To Heidegger, in doing so, individuals come to appreciate their location in the
world and the circumstances they find themselves in. Such acts of appreciation,
for the philosopher, were ways to feel at home, to reach accommodation with
one's surroundings. 'Dwelling' is reached in this sense of accommodation. This
term, discussed further below, is key to Heidegger's thinking about architecture.

Albert Hofstadter has written about Heidegger's motivation in attempting to
encapsulate existence in this way:

> In order to say what he must say, reporting what he sees, relaying what he
> hears, the author has to speak of gods, mortals, the earth [. . . This] is not
> abstract theorising about the problems of knowledge, value or reality; it is
> the most concrete thinking and speaking about Being, the differing being
> of different beings and the onefoldness of their identity in and with all their
> differences [. . .]. (1971: xi)

The fourfold, suggests Hofstadter, shows Heidegger trying to report human
existence as it seemed to him. He attempted to categorise what was around

him from the basis of his own involvement in the world. The four were offered as what he judged the most primary circumstances of existence, the inescapable pre-requisite of the world into which humans are 'thrown' without consent (1962, 164–168). They are his best guess at summarising the circumstances of the human condition. Against them one stands forth alone, distinguished by an impulse stemming from existence to make sense of existence. Some would argue that the fourfold demonstrates Heidegger, phenomenological reporter, at his most daring.

Heidegger's fourfold has been attributed to his interest in sources which include the mystic theologian Meister Eckhart, the Eastern philosopher Lao Tse already mentioned, and the poet Friedrich Hölderlin. However this fourfold does not readily fit the dialectical model of thinkers in rational discussion with one another. It is mythic and mystical, far from the strictures of logical thinking. It probably marks the moment of furthest distance on Heidegger's travels outward from conventional philosophy into free-fall writing from his own experience of his own being. Here is the thinker in his beloved Black Forest mountains, a long way from the library, with the landscape laid out before him.

Here is the thinker in his beloved Black Forest mountains, a long way from the library, with the landscape laid out before him.

George Steiner suggests that the fourfold is the manifestation of an 'ideolect'; a personal language offered as universal (1992, 9). Heidegger would refute this. If conceiving of the world around us through experience with reference to earth, sky, divinities and mortals appears rather unhinged to a contemporary Western mindset, then the philosopher would argue that it is our technocratic conception of the world which is unhinged and not his. What are received as truths through a scientific education and the institutional structures of society are, to him, just one outlook on the world. He found this outlook inadequate and countered it with another. Why is it necessarily stranger to consider our surroundings in terms of earth, sky, divinities and mortals than it is to consider them in terms of scientific progress, of human control, or of so-called rational logic? In advancing his argument about the thingness of his hypothetical jug judged according to the fourfold, Heidegger advocated an unashamedly mystical view of the world.

Gathering

The jug was, to Heidegger, primarily a thing because it 'gathered' ('*Versammeln*', carrying connotations of meeting and assembly). Again, the philosopher sought etymological authority, considering meanings of the word 'thing' (the English is derived from the same root as the German '*Ding*'). Heidegger recounted a history of meanings and interpretations of the word thing in Greek, Latin, English, Old High German and philosophical usage, finding the most important root as one shared with a root of the word 'gathering': '[. . .] *one* semantic factor in the old usage of the word *thing*, namely "gathering" does speak to the nature of the jug [. . .] [his emphasis]' (1971, 177). He felt that this etymological link provided evidence of what constituted thingness. For Heidegger, language recorded that a thing gathered what was around it for reflection. And what it gathered, through its existence and its use, was the fourfold: 'The presence of something present such as the jug comes into its own, appropriatively manifests and determines itself, only from the thinging of the thing' (1971, 177). Or, the jug and its corresponding void had the potential to contain, and embody, the fourfold preconditions of existence, holding in its familiarity the possibility of reflecting the fourfold back to those who engaged with it. For Heidegger, the specific example of the jug served as a broader example of the role of things in the world. In 'Building Dwelling Thinking', he attributed the same potential to buildings.

Being close to things

Having pursued several strands related to his argument, Heidegger attempted to draw them together, asking:

> **What is nearness? To discover the nature of nearness, we gave thought to the jug near by. We have sought the nature of nearness and found the nature of the jug as a thing. But in this discovery we also catch sight of the nature of**

nearness. The thing things. In its thinging, it stays earth and sky, divinities and mortals. Staying, the thing brings the four, in their remoteness, near to one another [. . .] Nearness brings near – draws nigh to one another – the far [*die Ferne*] [. . .] The thing is not 'in' nearness, 'in' proximity, as if nearness were a container. Nearness is at work in bringing near, as the thinging of the thing. (1971: 177–178)

This passage is the crux of Heidegger's argument. Here he is at his most rhetorical, his most intense and his most idiosyncratic. He is also at his most Heideggerian: it's this sort of prose which readers react to most strongly. Heidegger's point here is that nearness is a fundamental aspect of human experience. Experience of nearness may be appreciated through the tactile, cognitive and sociological familiarity of things. A thing is enmeshed in existence, bound with intricacies of life's daily experiences. Although it may be measured mathematically, it's primarily understood through experience of its use and the inward cognition of that experience. Such understanding brings a feeling of proximity to the world. For Heidegger, nearness means a sense of human relationship to the fourfold conditions of life.

The philosopher considered things to be unpretentious but important prompts in daily existence. Most of the time, people use things without thinking about them. But if, occasionally, they are thought about then they might also report something about an individual's relationship to the raw presence of their existence. Things have the potential to do this by mirroring their user, by orientating them in a reflection of earth, sky, divinities and mortals. Nearness thus becomes a function of immediacy: one is near to what one finds immediate, however far away it may be; and one is also far from that which one doesn't find immediate, however close it may be. For Heidegger, the definitive characteristic of a thing is its possibility to bring people nearer to themselves, to help them engage with their existence and the fourfold.

Nearness thus becomes a function of immediacy: one is near to what one finds immediate, however far away it may be.

Heidegger wrote 'The Thing' in 1950 with experience of the privations of the past five years in Germany: years of hunger, displacement and housing crisis. His discussion of things and objects is perhaps remarkable in this context. In his first public lecture following his rehabilitation, the philosopher didn't explicitly address any of what would seem, on the face of it, to be the foremost matters of concern to his contemporaries. Instead he explored what he considered to be primary relations between humans and what he judged the most basic constituents of existence.

'Building Dwelling Thinking'

Heidegger first presented 'Building Dwelling Thinking', *'Bauen Wohnen Denken'*, as a conference paper. It was published in the proceedings of the event and reprinted in the 1954 volume *Vorträge und Aufsätze* (*Lectures and Writings*). The philosopher avoided commas in his title to emphasise a unity he perceived between the three notions of building, dwelling and thinking. The conference – *'Mensch und Raum'*, 'Man and Space' – was held in Darmstadt from 4 to 6 August 1951, its audience consisting largely of architects, engineers and philosophers ([n.a], 1991). The discussion after Heidegger's paper was chaired by Otto Bartning who was head of the school of architecture in Weimar after the Bauhaus moved to Dessau and whose built projects included the Siemensstadt housing in Berlin. Other architects contributing to the event included: Paul Bonatz, designer of Stuttgart station in pre-Nazi Germany and an early influence on Walter Gropius; Richard Riemerschmid, who had been a key member of the *Jugendstil* movement; and Hans Scharoun, who later designed the Berlin Philharmonie and West German National Library. Other prominent delegates included sociologist Alfred Weber and philosophers Hans-Georg Gadamer and José Ortega y Gasset.

Heidegger's paper developed a number of themes that he had explored in 'The Thing'. He considered building and dwelling to be bound up intimately with one another. For him, these activities were related through people's involvement with the things of 'place'; and their attempts to make sense of place. 'Building

Dwelling Thinking' was structured around two questions: 'What is it to dwell?'; and 'How does building belong to dwelling?' (1971, 347). Heidegger claimed dwelling to be a peaceful accommodation between individuals and the world, integral with building through the fourfold conditions of existence, which he restated. The philosopher illustrated his argument with examples, particularly a bridge and an eighteenth century farmhouse. This farmhouse, for him, summarised how building and dwelling sustained the making and adaptation of places. Like 'The Thing', 'Building Dwelling Thinking' is characterised by etymological mining, rhetorical questioning and a distinctive density and circularity of prose.

Architecture is not enough

Heidegger felt that architects and historians tended to judge architecture more according to aesthetic priorities and less according to the priorities of people who make and inhabit places for themselves. To him, this was a cause for concern. He suggested that the word 'architecture' was part of the problem. He preferred instead to talk of building and dwelling. Heidegger wrote that:

> [. . .] thinking about building does not presume to discover architectural ideas, let alone give rules for building. (1971: 145)

Associating architecture with dictatorial rules for imagining and managing construction, he questioned the sort of architectural ideas (principles, guidance, policies) which are prepared by professionals for the consumption of other professionals. He suggested that:

> [. . .] the erecting of buildings cannot be understood adequately in terms of either architecture or engineering construction, nor in terms of a mere combination of the two. (1971: 159)

Heidegger's use of the word architecture in 'Building Dwelling Thinking' is thus almost pejorative.

Rich with memories of an ancient tradition, the word architecture is loaded with attitudes about what might or might not be counted as architecture.

Rich with memories of an ancient tradition, the word architecture is loaded with attitudes about what might or might not be counted as architecture. It recalls the historian Nikolaus Pevsner's dismissal of a bicycle shed as mere building and praise for Lincoln Cathedral as architecture (1963). Many architects and historians have, like Pevsner, followed philosophical aesthetics in perceiving architecture to be art. They have discussed relative merits of beauty in architecture and evolved systems in pursuit of ideal architectural form, from the classical orders to Le Corbusier's *Modulor* (1954). These are largely visual concerns whose recent primacy has been attributed to eighteenth century thought (Vesely 1985, 21–38). Especially at the time Heidegger wrote, many architecture books – and the habits of architectural historians – tended to emphasise the visual appreciation of buildings as decorated or stripped art objects (Arnold 2002, 83–126). Heidegger felt that this conception of architecture wasn't enough. To him, it devalued the all-important dimension of human inhabitation. The words building and dwelling, instead of the word architecture, allowed Heidegger to emphasise inhabitation and experience over the priorities of aesthetics.

Building and dwelling

Heidegger began 'Building Dwelling Thinking' by posing the question 'What is it to Dwell?' (1971, 145). He questioned certain contemporary ways of life in comparison with an imaginary past dwelling:

> Bridges and hangars, stadiums and power stations are buildings but not dwellings; railway stations and highways, dams and market halls are built, but they are not dwelling places. Even so, these buildings are in the domain of our dwelling. That domain extends over these buildings and yet is not limited to the dwelling place. The truck driver is at home on the highway,

but he does not have his shelter there; the working woman is at home in the spinning mill [!], but does not have her dwelling place there; the chief engineer is at home in the power station, but he does not dwell there. These buildings house man. He inhabits them and yet does not dwell in them. In today's housing shortage even this much is reassuring and to the good; residential buildings do indeed provide shelter; today's houses may even be well planned, easy to keep, attractively cheap, open to air, light and sun, but do the houses in themselves hold any guarantee that *dwelling* occurs in them? (1971: 145–146)

This paragraph echoes Heidegger's account of nearness in 'The Thing'. For him, one can occupy buildings daily but not feel at home in them or near to them. The philosopher chose his words carefully to outline the sorts of dwelling he found wanting, highlighting technocratic words of which he was critical. He implied that notions such as 'well planned', 'easy to keep' and 'attractively cheap' were missing the point of dwelling. He drew attention to terms like 'residential' and 'housing' which emphasise production systems over the priorities of human inhabitation. For Heidegger, this contemporary language offered a revealing commentary: it indicated a systemised building industry whereby a distant professional procures buildings for a market of unknown consumers. Heidegger challenged this notion of buildings as products for consumption: 'For building isn't merely a means and a way towards dwelling – to build is in itself already to dwell' (1971, 146). Contemporary relations between building and dwelling suggested to Heidegger an unfavourable comparison between past and present.

A more satisfactory relationship between building and dwelling was to be found for him in the etymology of those words. He suggested that they share the same root in old German (the English 'build' and 'dwell' also come from the same German root). This common origin was no coincidence to him. It indicated that 'building' and 'dwelling' were previously understood as one and the same activity (Heidegger's emphases):

Bauen originally means to dwell. Where the word *bauen* still speaks in its original sense it also says *how far* the essence of dwelling reaches. That is

> *bauen, buan, bhu, beo* are our word *bin* in the versions: *ich bin*, I am, *du bist*, you are, the imperative form *bis*, be. What then does *ich bin* mean? The old word *bauen* to which the *bin* belongs, answers: *ich bin, du bist* mean I dwell, you dwell. The way in which you are and I am, the manner in which we humans *are* on the earth, is *buan*, dwelling [. . .] The old word *bauen* which says that man *is* insofar as he *dwells*, this word *bauen*, however also means at the same time to cherish and protect, to preserve and to care for, specifically to till the soil, to cultivate the vine. (1971: 147)

There was a distinction to be made between two modes of building for Heidegger: building as construction, akin to the conventional definition; and building as nurturing. In German, *'bauen'* is the verb for to build and *'der Bauer'* is the noun for a farmer. Drawing from this etymology, the philosopher equated building with nurturing a seed into a plant. Moreover, Heidegger found the activity of building and dwelling, as combined together, to be central to language: it was present in 'I am', *'ich bin'*, which suggested to him that building and dwelling were once at the core of any affirmation of being. This etymology reported that whenever we say 'I am', 'you are', 'we are', we restate the importance of building and dwelling conceived together through human existence. To him, building and dwelling, as construction and cultivation, were vital to any acknowledgement of human existence in language.

. . . building and dwelling, as construction and cultivation, were vital to any acknowledgement of human existence in language.

After exploring the etymology of *'bauen'*, Heidegger explored the linked etymology of *'wohnen'*: dwelling (Heidegger's emphases):

> The Old Saxon *wuon*, the Gothic *wunian*, like the old word *bauen*, mean to remain, to stay in a place. But the Gothic *wunian* says more distinctly how this remaining is to be experienced. *Wunian* means to be at peace, to be brought to peace, to remain in peace. The word for peace, *Friede*, means

the free, das *Frye*; and *fry* means preserved from harm and danger, preserved
from **something, safeguarded. To free actually means to spare [. . .].**
(1971: 148–149)

Here Heidegger developed his discussion from 'The Thing' about dwelling as an
accommodation between people and their surroundings. Language suggested
to him that dwelling involved somehow being at one with the world: peaceful,
contented, liberating. It was connected to the mode of building that involves
cultivating and nurturing. He felt that the meaning of building and dwelling,
both as words and activities, had been lost.

Two examples might serve to explain Heidegger's conjoined notion of
building and dwelling. The first is a dining table. With conventional notions
of building and dwelling, an ordinary dining table might be thought to have
some relation with dwelling but little with building. Certain special tables could
be perceived as building or architecture perhaps, like those indispensable to the
dining room of a classical villa or the hall of an historic college, but domestic
dining tables would seldom be included. This seems to beg a question about
when a table might or might not be considered as architecture or building.
To Heidegger, however, any such question remains irrelevant. Building and
dwelling are always associated with any dining table – from those in baronial
halls to those in regular flats and houses – because the table necessarily
participates in daily life.

In Heidegger's scheme, using the table constitutes dwelling. And people's
engagement with it constitutes building and dwelling. Moving the table around
the room is building, of a sort, done in response to the needs of its users.
Likewise, laying out places for a meal is also a kind of building, organised
around how people anticipate eating there (Unwin 1997, 79). In this way,
dwelling (or human engagement with the table) is dependent upon building
(or the arrangement of the table, both as how it's located and how it's
organised for use). Similarly building is dependent on dwelling (the organisation
of the table follows how people want to engage with it). In Heideggerian terms,
here is the building of cultivation inextricably involved with dwelling in the daily
micro-organisation of eating meals.

The second example is a house occupied by a hypothetical family with a newborn child. In need of almost constant attention, the child will spend the first few weeks of its life with an adult or adults. It may sleep in a cot nearby so it can be given the attention it needs. But as the child grows, the adults might feel increasingly uncomfortable sharing their most intimate spaces, at least in Western cultures, and the child may then be given somewhere for themselves. This is a matter of dwelling. If the house can be rearranged to grant somewhere to the child, the solution is easy. If it can't be, an obvious solution is to extend the house. The issue then becomes a matter of building. In Heideggerian terms, dwelling requires building; building which responds to the needs of dwelling. To the philosopher, this would be the same activity as the arrangement and rearrangement of the dining table, but on a larger scale.

However, extending a house can be complex in contemporary Western society. Inhabitants will need to work within organisational structures established by professionals. They will have to work with contractors, planners, building control officers; and perhaps with mortgage lenders, surveyors, architects, engineers and quantity surveyors. Statutory permissions will be needed. An architect may be engaged. She or he might advise the employment of other consultants. Contracts will be signed. The unexpected, which inevitably accompanies building work, will have to be negotiated and paid for according to the terms of the contract. Professionals will speak an unfamiliar specialised vocabulary. In Heidegger's scheme, where building and dwelling were once related directly, their relationship has become distorted by the priorities of professionals. For the philosopher, vested interests have conspired to separate building from dwelling.

Heidegger's building and dwelling took place together over time. The activity described by these words wasn't so much the preserve of professionals as the way of life of regular people. It described individuals' ongoing relationship with the world around them at a variety of scales; taking place over months, years and lives. It wasn't the short-term outcome of a mercantile production process managed by experts. Making reference to the phrase 'plight of dwelling' describing the post-war shortage of West German homes, Heidegger suggested that it was this disruption of relations between building and dwelling, rather than the production of houses, that remained the most important plight in the contemporary world. He felt this plight lay with continuing attempts to rethink building and dwelling according to the expert priorities of technocratic society.

Heidegger suggested that it was this disruption of relations between building and dwelling, rather than the production of houses, that remained the most important plight in the contemporary world.

Building, dwelling and fourfold

To Heidegger, building and dwelling were interwoven with the fourfold that he had already written about in 'The Thing':

> The fundamental character of dwelling [. . .] reveals itself to us as soon as we reflect that human being consists in dwelling and, indeed, dwelling in the sense of mortals stay on the earth. But 'on the earth' already means 'under the sky'. Both of these *also* mean 'remaining before the divinities' and include a 'belonging to men's being with one another'. By a *primal* oneness the four – earth and sky, divinities and mortals – belong together in one. (1971: 149)

Having encountered it before, this fourfold now seems a little less strange.

Heidegger enjoyed the connotations of the German word '*Erde*', 'earth', which describes both soil and planet. It recalls an immediate sense of ground as planet, as open terrain stretching to the horizon. It can also refer to a particular place on earth and to dust, including the dust of mortality. Heidegger described 'earth', soil and planet together, as the 'serving bearer' (1971, 149). For him, it was the literal and metaphorical ground of existence. Meanings held by words such as earth and ground suggest multiple possibilities. No one can exist without the Earth. Subsistence involves fruits of the earth: plants and animals; also building materials including clay, wood, steel, aluminium, sand, lime, even oil-based plastics. Obeying conditions imposed by gravity, life grows, subsists, changes and adapts from the firm foundation of the earth. For Heidegger, the earth situates humans. In turn, humans remain at one with the earth. The philosopher challenged the perception that the earth is a commodity to be exploited. Pre-empting today's sustainability movement, he advocated that the earth be held in respect, not spoiled and subjugated.

For Heidegger, to be on the earth was also to be at one with the sky. Earth and sky remained interlocked for him as ever-present companions. The word 'sky' also suggested rich possibilities. Heidegger's account of sky referred to practicalities necessitated by weather. However, the German word '*Himmel*' can also mean 'Heaven' and he was conscious of the double meaning. To Heidegger, sky enveloped human existence. Night and day, changing seasons, wind, rain, snow and sun determine how people live and remain constant companions. The fickleness of wind, rain, snow and sun determine a basic need for shelter. Heidegger insisted that seasons and inclement weather should be accepted with grace. To him, we always exist with the bite of the wind, the chill of the snow, the cold saturation of rain and the burning intensity of the sun; and our absence of control over these forces hints at powers beyond our reach.

'Divinities', the third element of the four that Heidegger considered, remains the most problematic to a secular Western outlook. The dome of the sky in particular hinted at what might lie beyond. Hans-Georg Gadamer suggested that, for Heidegger, one might still 'call to the disappeared gods'; that to 'call' gods, to make use of the word gods, could invoke an absence that the word names (1994, 167–195). Through this naming, Gadamer argued, humans still have 'access to much of the divine' for Heidegger. This connection is more straightforward in German, where '*Göttlichen*' is to '*Gott*' just as gods is to God in English, but the adjective '*göttlich*' also exists – like the English divine – with religious associations and connotations of beauty and grace. Heidegger's '*Göttlichen*' thus refers simultaneously to gods and the divine. It has been suggested that the philosopher's talk of gods in the fourfold neither allowed nor disallowed any confessional outlook (Steiner 1992, 155). His 'beckoning messengers' of the divine stood instead for a mystical dimension of life that can't be rendered rational (1971, 150). To him, forces of nature, which remained a mysterious and humbling inspiration, allowed people to await the divinities.

'Mortals' were Heidegger's fourth integral element of the fourfold. The German word '*Sterblichen*' draws from '*sterblich*', mortal, and '*sterben*,' to die. Heidegger deliberately wrote in terms of mortals, rather than humans or beings, to emphasise his view that life persists in the face of its opposite, nothing, and always consists of 'Being-toward-Death' (Steiner 1992, 104–105). For Heidegger, time and mortality weren't inconveniences. Instead, they were to be respected and celebrated.

To Heidegger, the fourfold accommodated mortals. Earth, sky and divinities shaped daily life. In the shadow of mortality, they offered possibilities for celebrating existence, for rituals and rites of passage. Heidegger advocated that the mortal condition was, humbly, to 'save' the earth. Saving, for him, meant to set free. Mortals should 'receive' the sky, 'await' the divinities and 'initiate' their own being (1971, 150). These verbs – 'saving', 'receiving', 'awaiting' and 'initiating' – described how individuals should respond to the respective constituents of the fourfold. Heidegger judged that dwelling in this way contained a proper sense of order: a challenge to resist extending the tentacles of human control ever wider into the world. Here was his response to his own question: 'What is it to dwell?'

Elsewhere, the philosopher wrote of the piety of thinking (Heidegger, 1976). He used the word piety not in terms of smug self-restraint, as often interpreted today, but in reference to quietude: allowing and enabling what is already there. Just as a good interviewer or seminar tutor can initiate a conversation and then encourage it to proceed so they all but leave the room, piety for Heidegger listened to and facilitated the world around. Heidegger's discussion of the relationship of building and dwelling to the fourfold isn't so much about the piety of thinking as the piety of dwelling. The qualities he advocated of saving, receiving, awaiting and initiating are less about human will than a will-not-to-will.

Having related dwelling to the fourfold, Heidegger next turned to the second polemical question of 'Building Dwelling Thinking': 'In what way does building belong to dwelling?' He developed his claim that building and dwelling were once understood as one and the same activity, vitally connected with human presence in the world. A building shouldn't be understood just as an object to be admired or the product of a construction management process. Rather, it is primarily part of an ongoing human experience of building and dwelling. He reinforced this by describing a building as a 'built thing'.

As we've already considered, the word 'thing' in Heidegger's vocabulary describes life's paraphernalia immersed in experience and use, rather than distantly observed according to an abstract system. It was an alternative to the notion of object, which he found problematic. To him, a building wasn't a different object to a table: both were things, similar because they relate people to the fourfold in everyday life, helping people to orientate themselves in the world. For him, a built thing – like any thing – should be understood through tactile and imaginative experience; not as a detached object.

A building shouldn't be understood just as an object to be admired or the product of a construction management process. Rather, it is primarily part of an ongoing human experience of building and dwelling.

Heidegger gave an example: a hypothetical bridge. He suggested how the bridge might act as a thing in gathering and placing the fourfold. His choice of example contained the implicit suggestion that 'a building' might be any of the diverse outcomes of the act of 'building': referring not just to houses or schools or offices but to any variety of human interactions of building and dwelling, from furniture to cities. Heidegger's choice of a bridge also allowed him access to the etymology of the word '*Brücke*', bridge, which can speak of building bridges and bridging a divide. Heidegger's commentary on his hypothetical bridge is important, and is quoted here at length:

> The bridge swings over the stream 'with ease and power'. It does not just connect banks that are already there. The banks emerge as banks only as the bridge crosses the stream. The bridge expressly causes them to lie across from each other. One side is set off against the other by the bridge. Nor do the banks stretch along the stream as indifferent border strips of the dry land. With the banks, the bridge brings to the stream the one and the other expanse of the landscape ['*Uferlandschaft*'; with both picturesque and technical connotations] lying beyond them. It brings stream and bank and land into each other's neighbourhood. The bridge *gathers* the earth as landscape around the stream. Thus it guides and attends the stream through the meadows. Resting upright in the stream's bed, the bridge-piers bear the swing of the arches that leave the stream's waters to run their course. The waters may wander on quiet and gay, the sky's floods from storm or thaw may shoot past the piers in torrential waves – the bridge is ready for the sky's weather and its fickle nature. Even where the bridge covers ['*überdeckt*', 'roofs over'] the stream, it holds its flow up to the sky by taking it for a moment under the vaulted gateway and then setting it free once more.
>
> The bridge lets the stream run its course and at the same time grants mortals their way, so that they may come and go from shore to shore. Bridges initiate ['*geleiten*': 'to accompany' or 'to escort'] in many ways [. . .] Always and ever differently the bridge initiates the lingering and hastening ways of men to and fro, so that they may get to other banks and in the end, as mortals, to the other side. Now in a high arch, now in a low, the bridge vaults over glen and stream – whether mortals keep in mind the vaulting of the bridge's course or forget that they, always themselves on their way to the last bridge, are actually striving to surmount all that is common and unsound in them in order to bring themselves before the haleness of the divinities. The bridge *gathers*, as a passage that crosses [*überschwingende Übergang*], before the divinities – whether we explicitly think of and visibly *give thanks for*, their presence, as in the figure of the saint of the bridge, or whether that divine presence is obstructed or even pushed wholly aside.
> (1971: 152–153)

Although it also operates on the level of metaphor, Heidegger's hypothetical bridge was offered primarily as an example of an actual physical thing built as part of the world. In describing it, he wove together argument and method of inquiry, playing with the resonances of every word. In support of his case he offered multiple layers of meaning. Just as the jug was an opportune example for Heidegger's arguments about the possibilities of things, so the bridge was particularly conducive for discussing buildings. Its characteristics offered distinctive connections with the fourfold.

The bridge renegotiated the role of the river in the experience of nearby dwellers, for Heidegger, denying water its inherent possibility to prevent human occupation by allowing access over. He emphasised this seemingly obvious point:

> **The bridge is a thing and *only that*. Only? As this thing it gathers the fourfold. (1971: 153)**

The presence of the bridge, its being, had a far greater impact, for Heidegger, on people's immediate experience than it might first appear. In a technocratic appreciation of the world, building a bridge is not so much of a big deal: it might involve constructional, logistical and economic difficulties but it can be conceived with relative ease. However, to Heidegger, the building of a bridge had phenomenological significance much greater than the sum of its technical expediencies. The banks, in terms of mathematical distance, weren't far apart. However, with regard to the practicalities of access, they were. Without the bridge, people would have to walk or drive much further to get to the other bank. By allowing people to cross the water at that spot, the bridge changed irrevocably patterns of people's everyday lives: individuals could get to work more easily, new trade links might be forged, new friends made and lovers courted. Here is the difference between built object and built thing: as a primarily visual object, a bridge is something to be admired; but as a Heideggerian thing, the significance of a bridge consists in how its physical presence can influence the parameters of people's daily lives. Heidegger's rhetorical 'Only?' in the extract above suggests the significance he ascribed to this phenomenological reality.

Heidegger considered relationships between an individual and the fourfold. He felt that the hypothetical bridge allowed people to negotiate and renegotiate their relationship with earth, sky, divinities and mortals. When it was built, in the scheme of Heidegger's thinking, the bridge didn't just alter possibilities for life experience: it mediated between people and the world around them. The river was decked with material from the earth so as to join one lot of earth, one bank, to another lot of earth, the other bank. And the bridge allowed people to stand on earth above sky, above the void beneath the bridge. The spot under the bridge allowed people to stand between earth and earth, with earth separating them from sky, offering shelter. For Heidegger, it was no trivial matter that the bridge, and all buildings, altered relationships between individuals, earth and sky. If the world is imagined as the earth of Heidegger's fourfold before buildings had been made – earth as planet, as a surface extending to the horizons – then human existence at that mythical time involved people in a definite relationship with earth and sky: they stood on one, underneath the other. In the philosopher's implied story, buildings changed this relationship for human benefit by reconfiguring earth and sky, providing shelter and keeping out extremes of weather. The primary function of shelter enables dwelling. It makes civilisation possible. To Heidegger, much contemporary human activity relied on the power of shelter, and commonly ignored its power in enabling human endeavours.

Heidegger also suggested that the bridge might affect how an individual understood their situation. He felt that the bridge, as a Heideggerian thing, allowed people to negotiate and renegotiate their relationships with the world. People near the bridge, who cross it regularly or live near it, come to feel that they somehow understand it. It becomes familiar. And through its familiarity, the bridge offers people opportunities to relate themselves to the world around. For Heidegger, the bridge 'holds up' the individual. That phrase was meant both literally and metaphorically. To him, the bridge is a like a picture frame. It presents what crosses it. It also presents the world around the bridge to people crossing it. The bridge is intellectually significant because its presence allows people to understand the world around them in relation to it.

To him, the bridge is a like a picture frame. It presents what crosses it. It also presents the world around the bridge to people crossing it.

The bridge was a special place, perhaps even a sacred place for Heidegger, because bridge crossing enabled speculations of thought, locating experience with respect to the divinities. For Heidegger, daily physical bridge crossing doesn't necessarily involve thinking about being. But, as a thing which negotiates between people and their circumstances, the bridge might occasionally prompt people to think about being. It has latent potential to remind people about the fundamental power of their existence in the world.

Defining place in German and in English

Heidegger developed his discussion of the bridge in order to introduce the notion of place. The key passages on place in 'Building Dwelling Thinking' are significantly influenced by the English translation. Before exploring Heidegger's approaches to a definition of place, a brief note on translation is needed.

In German, one of Heidegger's decisive paragraphs on place in 'Building Dwelling Thinking' reads as follows (his italics):

> Raum, Rum, heißt freigemachter Platz für Siedlung und Lager. Ein Raum ist etwas Eingeräumtes, Freigegebenes, nämlich in eine Grenze, griechisch 'peras'. Die Grenze ist nicht das, wobei etwas [. . .] sein Wesen beginnt [. . .] Raum ist wesenhaft das Eingeräumte, in seine Grenze Eingelassne [. . .] Demnach empfangen die Räume ihr Wesen aus Orten und nicht aus <<dem>> Raum. (1997: 148)

This is rendered in English as:

> *Raum, Rum,* means a place cleared or free for settlement and lodging. A space is something that has been made room for, something that is cleared

and free, namely within a boundary, Greek *peras*. A boundary is not that at which something stops but [. . .] the boundary is that from which something *begins its presencing* [. . .] Space is in essence that for which room has been made, that which is let into its bounds [. . .] *Accordingly, spaces receive their being from locations, not from 'space'*. (1971: 154)

In the German text of 'Building Dwelling Thinking', Heidegger writes of '*Ort*,' '*Platz*' and '*Raum*'. In the English, '*Ort*', '*Platz*' and '*Raum*' are rendered as 'location', 'place' and 'space' respectively. This presents difficulties. '*Ort*' is the closest equivalent of the English word 'place', rather than 'location', because 'place' suggests the same sense of rootedness and immediacy. However, Heidegger also used the German word '*Platz*', which is also best translated as 'place' although it is perhaps closer to 'site' or 'area'. Because it shares the same root as the English, the translator chose, understandably, to render '*Platz*' as 'place' but this causes a problem when he translates '*Ort*'. For '*Ort*' he is forced to substitute 'location'. The philosopher's argument here – to which we will return in detail below – concerns a distinction between space and place, where 'spaces' gain authority not from 'space' appreciated mathematically but 'place' appreciated through human experience. The key word in the sentence is '*Orten*': 'places'. But the translation muddies the issue because of the convention of translating '*Ort*' as 'location' and '*Platz*' as 'place'. Although Heidegger was hostile to the English language, it appears that English would have been more helpful than German to him in dealing with place because the English word encompasses relevant meanings of both '*Ort*' and '*Platz*'.

. . . a distinction between space and place, where 'spaces' gain authority not from 'space' appreciated mathematically but 'place' appreciated through human experience.

Another point about translation is worth raising. 'Place' in English has a verb form – 'to place' – which neither '*Ort*' nor '*Platz*' have in German. In English, a place can become a place because of the action and understanding of placing. '*Raum*', 'space', does have a verb form in German but Heidegger needed to avoid that for the sake of his argument. Instead, he referred to '*versammeln*', a verb discussed above with respect to 'The Thing', which Hofstädter translated as 'to gather'. There is a credible case that when Heidegger talks about something 'gathering', it might also be translated to English as 'placing'. This possibility doesn't exist in German but it reflects the philosopher's broader point; he refers to things being placed in the world according to human experience.

In what follows, then, I will amend the standard translation. I will talk about place in the wider sense encompassing both '*Ort*' and '*Platz*', and also use the verb 'to place'. This convention corresponds with discussions of place in the English language texts of architectural Heideggerians, such as Christian Norberg-Schulz (1971, 1980, 1988) and David Seamon (1989, 1993).

How a place happens

Rather than consider place through another etymological investigation, Heidegger explored it in connection with his hypothetical bridge:

> **The [place] is not already there before the bridge is. Before the bridge stands, there are of course many spots along the stream that can be occupied by something. One of them proves to be a [place], and does so because of the bridge. Thus the bridge does not come first to a [place] to stand in it; rather a [place] comes into existence only by virtue of the bridge. (1971: 154)**

For Heidegger, places, like things and buildings, were primarily understood through use and experience. To him, the spot where the bridge was sited was understood differently once the bridge was built. It became in peoples' minds the place of the bridge.

In this extract, Heidegger offered a story about the origin of the bridge, imagining how it was before the bridge was built. The key moment of this originary myth was the moment that the bridge builder chose the spot for its location. That moment was crucial for Heidegger, and architectural writers have discussed it following his thinking: Christian Norberg-Schulz has called it the 'concretization' of space (1971, 6) and Simon Unwin refers to it as the 'identification of place' (1997, 13–17). Whatever it might be termed, this is for Heidegger the moment that dwelling is inscribed in place through building. There would have been reasons, in Heidegger's story, why the builder chose the particular spot on the bank. Perhaps undulations of river and bank were conducive to building there. Perhaps it was the easiest spot to defend from invaders. Whatever the reasons, it was judged the most appropriate spot to place a bridge. And once the bridge was built, that spot became in people's understanding the place of the bridge. The initial identification of place was, through building, adopted by others and absorbed into their understanding.

. . . this is for Heidegger the moment that dwelling is inscribed in place through building.

A picnic in a park might serve as an example of the identification of place (Unwin 1997, 15). Picnickers will look for a good place to sit. If it's a fine day, they might want to sit in the sun or prefer a patch of shade. They might want to look at other people in the park: in the hope of seeing friends; to idly watch a game of sport; or from sheer nosiness. They might want an expansive view, or choose a more secluded spot. The picnickers will dither and debate until they find somewhere which serves everyone's whims. An identification of place thus occurs. If they're well prepared, our picnickers may next lay out a picnic blanket. There may be a debate about how to arrange the blanket – long side to the view or to the road? – and with agreement another identification of place is made. Then people will choose where to sit: the nosiest might choose the best corner for people-watching; acquaintances who dislike each other will choose opposite ends of the blanket; someone might hurry to sit next to someone else. Each of these choices also involves identifying a place. Last, our picnickers will lay out their food: the hamper in the middle, maybe; the hard-boiled eggs in easy reach of the egg lover; a drinker hoarding the beer. The organisation of the picnic is a choreography of small-scale place identifications. In Heideggerian terms a site has been gathered; the picnic has been placed. Numerous places have come into existence by virtue of the picnic.

When the meal is packed away and gone, the place of the picnic might live on in the minds of the picnickers. If lovers first kindled their interest in one another at the picnic, perhaps, or if a memorable announcement was made, or if something especially funny or unusual happened, then those involved would never look at the same corner of the park in the same way. The site of the picnic wouldn't be just ground; it would be remembered as where *that* picnic took place. The memory might last for many years. It could even be passed down between generations: 'that was where Grandma . . .' In Heideggerian terms, the place wasn't there before the picnic was. But for those on whose minds the picnic became imprinted, it would always be identified as the place of the picnic. Others, who maybe have cause to identify instead with other places in the park, could pass it every day with no appreciation of the picnic and the place that other people recognise.

For Heidegger, this example wouldn't be trivial. It illustrates activities of place identification which, to him, remained constantly in play, shaping the organisation of rooms, buildings, towns and cities. In this Heideggerian scheme, the choices which locate a house in a landscape are not so different to those involved in arranging a picnic blanket in a park. If a house is located and built in such a landscape, outbuildings might later be configured around it, involving other identifications of place. In time, a neighbouring house might be added, then another house, a street, another street, then a village and over time a town or even a city. Cities, especially if not planned, might be said to record many millions of place identifications in their layout, most of them long forgotten like the people who made them and the reasons for which they were made.

The world, for Heidegger, is parcelled up into intersecting places of many sorts, sizes, shapes and scales; identified by individuals and kept to themselves or shared. Gloriously, according to the philosopher's outlook, activities involving the identification of place are neither logical nor systematic; remaining subjective, tentative, shifting and contingent.

For Heidegger, the intellectual demarcation of somewhere 'admitted' the fourfold:

> The bridge is a thing; it [places] the fourfold, but in such a way as it allows a site for the fourfold. By this site are determined the [places] and ways by which a space is provided for. (1971: 154)

For the philosopher, the demarcation of somewhere for a specific purpose – the identification of a place – marked out a particular human alignment with earth, sky, divinities and mortals. Intellectual demarcation could be fulfilled by physical demarcation: construction. To Heidegger, construction – as making a building or just as the arrangement of a picnic blanket or a dining table – installs the fourfold by giving it presence. The place identified by one person can also become a place for others because of its physical incarnation. The existence of the identifier is reflected in their act of bringing a place into existence. Moreover, the act of construction arranges earth and sky (from which those materials are derived), mortals (whom the building allows to occupy the world in new ways) and divinities (upon whom mortals might reflect) as they weren't arranged before. For Heidegger, an individual understands building and dwelling through a matrix of place perceptions: 'Building thus characterised is a distinctive letting-dwell'.

The edges of places

Heidegger expanded on this notion of a place as a somewhere by considering how the edges of places might be determined (Heidegger's italics):

> *Raum* means a place cleared or free for settlement and lodging. A space is something that has been made room for, something that is cleared and free, namely within a boundary, Greek *peras*. A boundary is not that at which something stops but, as the Greeks recognised, the boundary is that from which something *begins its presencing.* That is why the concept is that of *horismos*, that is, the horizon, the boundary. Space is [. . .] that for which room has been made, that which is let into its bounds. That for which room [*Raum*] is made is always granted, and hence is joined, that is, [placed], by virtue of a [place], that is, by such a thing as the bridge. *Accordingly spaces receive their being from* [places] *and not from 'space'.* (1971: 154)

Space, for Heidegger, is parcelled up into places by people through the manifold identifications of place involved in their daily lives. To him, people's understanding of space is dependant on their experiences of the places they identify for themselves within the broader context of the generic 'space' surrounding us. Identifying a place involves determining a boundary of some sort around a place in space. This identification, as we have seen, belongs primarily in the mind of the beholder for Heidegger. By this means, places are made particular by individuals – in complex and ever shifting ways – within the generality of space. For him, only thus is space itself understood: as the context within which we're able to identify boundaries around places. To Heidegger space only comes into being because we're able to identify places.

. . . places are made particular by individuals – in complex and ever shifting ways – within the generality of space.

This point is vital to Heidegger's model of understanding the world around us, and the built world in particular. In his scheme, when we identify a place – like a place where a picnic happened – we do so by putting a boundary around it in our mind. It is as if we lassoo a somewhere out of the generic nowhere of space. The boundary isn't necessarily exact though, like a line drawn on a plan or like the rope of a lassoo. It could correspond with precise physical features, but it might also be more vague and indeterminate. In Heidegger's model, the edges of the places we define are more likely to be precise if they align with physical boundaries. Ready-made boundaries are often already there – a wall, a path, a river, a building, a kerbstone, a change in surface – and it's easy to identify places according to these demarcations which are pre-inscribed in the world for us. However there are some boundaries that it's less easy to be exact about.

Cities offer numerous examples of indeterminate edges to places; and you might recall some from your own experiences. For example, a street can have very different characters along its length: like the street where I live in Cardiff which connects a busy shopping road with a tree-lined avenue along the edge of a park. The shopping road feels frantic, with competing streams of traffic and pedestrians. The avenue at the other end is quieter, residential, dominated by mature lime trees. The character of my street changes noticeably along its length. Nearer the shops it feels busier and more urban; nearer the avenue it feels more genteel and suburban. Although terraced houses in the street were built almost identically, they too seem to change along its length; front gardens are tidier and the paintwork is neater at the park end. Considered according to Heidegger's scheme, the park end of my street feels like a different place to the shop end because its character seems so different. My neighbours seem to sense the same. So do estate agents, because the houses nearer the park end are more expensive, and the price difference is greater than that attributable to neater paint and gardens. I'm unable, however, to identify a line at which one end of the street becomes the other end. Here, in Heideggerian terms, is an identification of place which has no easily drawn boundary. The boundary is there, somewhere, because two distinct places seem apparent in experience. But while I can draw on a plan the line between gardens of houses and the street – because it corresponds to walls which are already there – it seems impossible to demarcate the places of each end of the street with a line.

Heidegger wrote of horizons when discussing the boundaries that he felt people identify around places. He was allowing for the sorts of edges that can't be represented easily on a plan drawing, like the difference between the two ends of my street. He referred to the more indeterminate edges that people perceive around places. A horizon is where earth meets sky, but it can't be located precisely in space. It's impossible to get to the horizon. If you walk towards it, it recedes into the distance. Like the fabled pot of gold at the end of the rainbow, the horizon only ever slips further away. While some boundaries of place identifications accord with physical things and can be recognised precisely, others are horizons in this sense. They're chimeras which can't be pinned down readily. For Heidegger, individuals know such boundaries by experience but can't locate them exactly. They can't be recorded with a line on a drawing but remain vital in people's identifications of place.

Heidegger wrote of horizons when discussing the boundaries that he felt people identify around places. He was allowing for the sorts of edges that can't be represented easily on a plan drawing.

This chimeric notion of horizon was about more than the edges of places for Heidegger. It also served as a metaphor for the contexts in which people appreciate things, themselves and others. In English, we talk about someone's horizons as the convictions which determine their appreciation of the world, and in the same way we talk about someone broadening their horizons. Heidegger also referred to horizons in this sense: key lessons learnt from someone's formal education, from everyday life, from family, from familiar or memorable surroundings. For the philosopher, all these things are horizons of a sort. And, to him, the fourfold of earth, sky, divinities and mortals was the ultimate horizon. Such horizons comprise the real or imagined presences which allow someone to identify with themselves, and from this basis to identify with the world around them. Just as the horizon between earth and sky can't be known in an exact way, nor can these broader metaphorical horizons. For Heidegger, the elusiveness of such horizons betrayed the ultimate mysteriousness of life. This mystery was to be celebrated. It demonstrated for him a vital preserve of experience in a technocratic world which he felt was dominated by claims made about the authority of mathematical systems.

Valuing experience over mathematics

Having proposed space as the context in which people identify places for themselves and explored how such identifications might happen, Heidegger next pitted his notion of place and space against the conception of space as described in mathematical increment. He continued with the example of the bridge:

The bridge is a [place]. As a thing, it allows a space into which earth and heaven, divinities and mortals, are admitted. The space allowed by the bridge contains many places variously near or far from the bridge. These places, however, may be treated as mere positions between which there lies a measurable distance [. . .]. As distance or 'stadion' it is what the same word, *stadion*, means in Latin, a *spatium*, an intervening space or interval. Thus nearness and remoteness between men and things can become mere distance, mere intervals of intervening space. In a space that is represented purely as *spatium*, the bridge now appears as a mere something at some position, which can be occupied at any time or replaced by a mere marker. What is more, the mere dimensions of height, breadth, and depth can be abstracted from space as intervals. (1971: 155)

The philosopher's argument is related to his opposition between object and thing. He judged that phenomenological appreciation, which emphasises ways that people experience places, offers a richer way to describe the world than mathematical abstraction.

The mathematical description of movement serves as an illustration. Distance is often graded three-dimensionally in equal increments on x, y and z axes. No differentiation is made between the description of vertical movement up and down from horizontal movement along the ground plane. Yet this is a very different situation from human experience (Bloomer and Moore 1977, 1–2). Without gradients or mechanical assistance, it isn't possible to move up very far because 'up' usually consists of air and gravity pins one's body to the ground. Equally, 'down' is generally earth, pushing the body upwards with similar force. To move up or down feels very different from moving along the ground in any direction. For Heidegger, mathematical description missed the point. Moving along the ground was clearly easier than moving up or down. Although they were the same mathematically, they were hugely different in human experience. Such demonstrations, for Heidegger, indicated that mathematical measuring couldn't cope with appreciating distance. To him, space and place should be understood first and foremost according to the human experience of building and dwelling, not mathematics.

Continuing the argument, Heidegger wrote:

> What is so abstracted [in space conceived as dimension] we represent as the pure manifold of the three dimensions. Yet the room made by this manifold is also no longer determined by distances; it is no longer a *spatium*, but now no more than *extensio* – extension. But from space as *extensio* a further abstraction can be made, to analytic-algebraic relations. [. . .] The space thus provided for in this mathematical manner may be called 'space', the 'one' space as such. But in this sense 'the' space, 'space', contains no spaces and no places. We never find it in any [places], that is, things of the kind the bridge is [. . .] *Spatium* and *extensio* afford at any time the possibility of measuring things and what they make room for, according to distances, spans, and directions, and of computing these magnitudes. But the fact that they are *universally* applicable to everything that has extension can in no case make numerical magnitudes the ground of spaces and locations that are measurable with mathematics. (1971: 155–156)

Heidegger's challenge to the measurement of space in mathematical increments – and its implicit project to universalise human experience of the world as dimensions on the x, y and z axes – was part of a broader challenge to the infiltration of scientific language into daily life.

He asked what would follow if the scientific project were completed: if a mathematical formula for life were written? Would everything then be known about life?

The philosopher also considered the pervasiveness of scientific language in his 1935 essay 'What is Metaphysics?' (1993). He suggested that science questions by asking 'what is?' He attempted to explore being by questioning its alternative: nothing. We have already encountered the philosopher's mythologizing of nothing with respect to his example of the jug in 'The Thing'. To Heidegger, contemporary language, which has been infiltrated by science, has a tendency to couch nothing in terms which render it as a hollow something. It can only ever describe a pale something and never a properly mysterious absence. For him, nothing is that most worthy of questioning; a shorthand for '[. . .] all that is dark and riddlesome in existence' (1993, 91). One cannot ask 'what is?' of nothing, precisely because it isn't anything. For Heidegger, science could never answer why there is not nothing because it takes human existence for granted.

Heidegger extended this argument in a 1969 essay 'The End of Philosophy and the Task of Thinking' (1993). He asked what would follow if the scientific project were completed: if a mathematical formula for life were written? Would everything then be known about life? Would motivation for human intellectual endeavour remain? He found continuing value in intuitive aspects of human existence, aspects that scientific language couldn't help with. He considered that the expansion and enrichment of life wouldn't cease in art, poetry and other means of expression should the scientific project ever be completed. There would still be much thinking to be done. For Heidegger, continuing merit was to be found in this realm of emotions and experiences.

Such experiences, to the philosopher, were crucial to human identifications of place. For him, technology obscured being on an everyday basis by dulling reminders of human frailty inherent in the world around. Such reminders appeal to the emotions. They might be considered by imagining feelings surrounding the death of a loved one, or an encounter on the brink of nature's forces. These spring from angst, anxiety, despair, imagination, and delight. Heidegger suggested that their prompts were diminished by a technocratic society and its language. They were regarded, wrongly, as occasional lapses to be dealt with as quickly as possible so that 'normality' might be regained. For him, this is a damaging substitute for a daily emotional response to the subtlety and might of the world. Bound into that emotional realm was the matrix of place identifications that people carry with them. Broadly, for Heidegger, the scientific project, and its tendency toward mathematical abstraction, was inadequate because it failed to address the daily implications of emotion. The appreciation of space following the mathematical increments of dimension was, for Heidegger, an unwelcome symptom of this flawed reduction.

There are important implications of Heidegger's model for understanding the world through individual experience in preference to numerical abstraction. Mathematical scale, according to which most maps and drawings are measured, is an immensely powerful tool. Construction, navigation and much in contemporary human imagination depend upon it. Heidegger, however, implied that scalar mathematical measure had accrued too much influence. It was implicated in what he felt was a seductive illusion that humans could take control over the world. It could prompt a reliance on the visual and abstract. In an architectural context it allowed all too easily for the conception of buildings as objects, where he believed that human feelings should instead stake the first claim. In the philosopher's scheme, the mathematical measurement of space was a tool rather than an end in itself. Beyond it was the way in which individuals perceive the world, as it seems to them, in terms of places.

Projecting places

As discussed above, Heidegger implied that people identify places for themselves by lassooing boundaries around them in their minds: some boundaries sharp and exact; some more tentative and provisional. For him, the ongoing identification of places at a variety of scales involved individuals in sensitivities of emotion and experience. Intuitive and shifting, such identification activities resisted reduction to the mathematical measurement of precise control. Crucially, to him, they involved people's imagination.

Heidegger explored the role of imagination in identifying places:

> We do not represent distant things merely in our mind [. . .] so that only mental representations of distant things run through our minds and heads as substitutes for the things. If all of us now think, from where we are right here, of the old bridge in Heidelburg, this thinking toward that location is not mere experience inside the persons present here; rather it belongs to the nature of our thinking *of* that bridge that *in itself* thinking gets through, persists through, the distance to that [place. . .] From right here we may even be much nearer to that bridge and to what it makes room for than

someone who uses it daily as an indifferent bridge crossing [. . .] When I go toward the door of the lecture hall, I am already there, and I could not go to it at all if I were not such that I am there. I am never here only, as this encapsulated body; rather, I am there, that is, I already pervade the room, and thus I can only go through it. (1971: 156–157)

Heidegger talked about the old bridge in Heidelburg, offering a specific example to stand in for the hypothetical bridge that he'd discussed in the essay thus far. This structure is famous in Germany. Heidegger knew that many in his audience would have visited it and could summon it up in their minds' eyes just as – if called to – a British audience could picture Tower Bridge in London or an Australian audience could picture the Sydney Harbour Bridge. In accordance with his definition of a thing, as opposed to the notion of an object, the philosopher wanted to challenge the suggestion that an object is primarily imagined as a pure mental image, as a visual ideal. He tried to play on the memories of his audience as individuals; to persuade them that they imagined the old bridge in Heidelburg first and foremost as a thing that they had experienced. He wanted them to consider it as a place remembered in association with their own experiences rather than as an ideal object. For Heidegger, imagining a place involves someone in projecting themselves to it through their imagination. To him, thinking of the old bridge in Heidelburg, or a picnic where something special happened, or your dining table at home, is to remember experiences of the bridge or the picnic or the table. For the philosopher, it involves an imaginative projection from here and now, to there, in our minds. We reach for an appreciation of the reality of the place and what it means to us emotionally by experience, rather than conjure an image which is primarily visual.

In Heidegger's scheme, this imaginative projection might involve us in thinking of a place's memorable qualities, memorable events that have happened there, memorable people associated with it, even memorable fictions we have made up about it. In this way, he claimed, we become near to places. Here he recalled his discussion of nearness in 'The Thing', related to the fourfold conditions of life. To him, nearness wasn't primarily a function of mathematical increment. Rather, it was a sense of emotional attachment to somewhere, something or someone – born of experience and inhabitation – understood in the context of earth, sky, divinities and mortals. Heidegger claimed that one could feel near to something far away, and far from something close at hand. In this way, imaginary places, lost places or places not yet visited might be as immediate as actual tangible locations. Those places are still identified according to the same framework, through the mind engaging with the world. But, in Heidegger's terms, they're a long way into the realm of boundary as horizon; their edges exist primarily in the mind rather than in accordance with sited physical things. Some elderly people for example, particularly those with failing sight and hearing, can have a lively proximity to places which changed out of all recognition many years ago and to long-dead people who inhabited them. They're sometimes nearer to those places and people in imaginative projection than they are to their current time and situation. Such remoteness from the pressures of the present can worry those of us more bound up in here and now; but to Heidegger's way of thinking this isn't necessarily a failing, instead a different sense of proximity.

Some elderly people for example, particularly those with failing sight and hearing, can have a lively proximity to places which changed out of all recognition many years ago and to long-dead people who inhabited them.

For Heidegger, our navigation of the places surrounding us relates as much to the projective identification of places – those appreciated through imagination and memory – as to identifications of place that accord with the immediate physical enclosures of buildings, streets and landscapes. The horizons of the world that each individual carries with them, for Heidegger, is constituted in richly changing ways understood through experience and inhabitation: some places rational, immediate and physically bounded; others more intuitive, indeterminate and imaginative. Everyone's individual sense of proximity, for him, is in constant negotiation between physical situation and imagination.

Heidegger concluded 'Building Dwelling Thinking' with a last example: a hypothetical farmhouse from the Black Forest of southern Germany. The house was offered as a summation of the text, integrating the key components of his argument: a conjoined building and dwelling already entwined with the things of the world; an opposition to architecture conceived as the production of art objects; the idiosyncratic fourfold of earth, sky, divinities and mortals offered as the first circumstance of existence which building and dwelling fulfil; the notion of place offered to explain how people demarcate the world around them; and a damning commentary on the technocratic outlook which he felt oversold mathematically-oriented systems and underplayed the priority of individual human feelings and experiences. Wary of what he perceived as the focus of architecture on production and the primacy of the visual, Heidegger introduced the Black Forest farmhouse by claiming: [his italics] *'Only if we are capable of dwelling, only then can we build'* (1971, 160).

A Black Forest farmhouse near Heidegger's hut at Todtnauberg, now used as a hotel.

... a damning commentary on the technocratic outlook which he felt oversold mathematically-oriented systems and underplayed the priority of individual human feelings and experiences.

The Black Forest farmhouse can be described, in the parlance of the object-focussed architectural history which Heidegger distrusted, as a 'vernacular building type'. Historians categorise these houses according to a number of characteristics. An outsize hipped roof, with eaves low to the ground, encloses a volume maybe four storeys tall, the size of the roof contrived to cope with heavy snow in winter [see above]. A relatively small proportion of the plan was given to human habitation, the remainder providing livestock accommodation and storage for hay and other necessities. This allowed humans and animals to share heat in severe mountain winters and to use the thermal mass of stored materials to retain as much warmth as possible. Construction is largely timber framed and timber shingle hung to both roof and walls. The largest room of the house is almost always a dining room, centred on the table called the *Familientisch* or *gemeinsamer Tisch* where family and extended family met to eat. Overlooking this, in the corner of the room, is a Catholic shrine likely to contain an icon and candles. This is the *Herrgottswinkel*, the 'Lord's Corner', beneath which the father would sit at mealtimes as head of the family. The Catholic faith and traditional family roles were strictly observed at such houses in the past. Many farmhouses also had a *Totenbrett* or *Totenbaum* outside: a partially buried log with a flat upper surface used as a coffin rest in the event of a family death.

Heidegger's account of the hypothetical Black Forest farmhouse draws in part from his own experience of his neighbours' houses around his mountain hut at Todtnauberg:

Let us think for a while of a farmhouse in the Black Forest [*einen Schwarzwaldhof*], which was built some two hundred years ago by the dwelling of peasants [*bäuerliches Wohnen*]. Here the self-sufficiency of the power to let earth, sky, divinities and mortals enter *in simple oneness* into things ordered the house. It [placed] the farm on the wind-sheltered mountain slope, looking south, among the meadows close to the spring. It gave it the wide overhanging shingle roof whose proper slope bears up under the burden of snow, and that, reaching deep down, shields the chambers against the storms of the long winter nights. It did not forget the altar nook behind the dining table [*gemeinsamen Tisch*]; it made room in its chamber for the sacred places of childbed and 'tree of the dead' [*Totenbaum*], for that is what they call a coffin there, and in this way it drafted for the different generations under one roof the sense of their journey through time. A craft that, itself sprung from dwelling, still uses its tools and gear as things, built the farmhouse.

Only if we are capable of dwelling, only then can we build. Our reference to the Black Forest farm in no way means that we should or could return to building such houses; rather it illustrates by a dwelling that *has been* how it was able to build. (1971: 160)

Heidegger felt that building and dwelling were in harmony at this hypothetical house. He appears to have understood the building as part of a dynamic whole set out by the occupants' routines; and by the physical and social micro-organisation of those routines in relation to locality and climate. Heidegger's passage on the farmhouse is dense with meaning and it is worth paying attention to details of his argument.

The farmhouse, Heidegger wrote, 'was built [. . .] by the dwelling of peasants'. He inverted the conventional expectation that building is a one-off event which is then followed by dwelling. The philosopher invoked his suggestion that building and dwelling instead remain conjoined as a single ongoing activity. The needs of dwelling at that place – in terms of site and climate, but also in terms of what was required to sustain everyday life – were decisive in planning the house. The needs of dwelling set out how, over time, the house was built, rebuilt, changed and adapted at a variety of scales from macro to micro; including everything from new extensions to the arrangement of the dining table. There was no distinction between building and dwelling, no claim to any sort of completion. In a reciprocal arrangement, the places of the building also determined much about how dwelling was configured there.

It was particularly through the unity of its residents' thoughts and deeds, Heidegger claimed, that dwelling gave rise to the configuration of the farmhouse. The building gathered together earth, sky, divinities and mortals – placing them – and the fourfold was fulfilled by the ways in which its residents dwelt. The farmhouse stood 'on the earth' and 'beneath the sky', made by the first dwellers there using materials garnered from the immediate surroundings. The building's timbers, shingles and stones were derived from earth, their origins also involving light and heat from the sky. Understanding how biting the wind could be, Heidegger's hypothetical dwellers chose a spot where its force was naturally diminished by the lie of the land. Realising that earth was an insulator able to mitigate extremes of temperature, they built close into the mountain slope. Feeling the sun's warmth, and seeing how its light penetrates, they turned the principal face southwards towards it. They worked the land, cultivating 'earth' whose crops and animals offered sustenance, choosing to build near the ground which provided for them. Like their crops and animals, they drew water from springs tapping the earth, and dwelt close by. In another inversion, it was the fourfold, and not the residents themselves, that ultimately 'ordered the house' for Heidegger. Human agency (people's control over their actions) wasn't in overall charge here, only working in negotiation with the fourfold. To the philosopher, it was vital that the residents of the farmhouse, the building and the landscape were self-sufficient: not in some hippie fantasy of dropping out, but as a source of meaning – whatever that may mean – reached through what he felt were appropriate mediations between people, their lifestyles, the locality and the planet. In this morality, the powers of nature are greater than the individual.

The farmhouse, for Heidegger, allowed privileged contact with the primacy of being. Its residents marked out their mortality through rites of passage and routines of daily existence.

The farmhouse, for Heidegger, allowed privileged contact with the primacy of being. Its residents marked out their mortality through rites of passage and routines of daily existence. They made certain special locations in the house where celebrations of the passing of years, and of birth and death in particular, might take place: the dining table, coffin rest and Lord's corner.

The *gemeinsamer Tisch*, in Heidegger's scheme, was set for particular, almost ceremonial, configurations of meals. The changing layout of the table traced those who met there over time and celebrated their meeting by sharing food. It announced the being of its diners; empty seats between meals awaiting the return of their regular incumbents. It was organised and cleared for every meal; plates, glasses and cutlery laid for each diner, used and washed-up. Places were set for people and things within the wider place of the dining table. These were regularly organised and occupied or, in Heidegger's parlance, built according to the needs of dwelling and dwelt according to configurations of building. The *Totenbaum* likewise awaited occupation: for Heidegger both a constant reminder of lives ultimately lived toward death and a presence reminding the family of ancestors whose lives culminated there. The *Herrgottswinkel*, whose Catholic icon supervised the dining table, likewise marked the passage of time. To Heidegger, the unchanging rites and rituals that it demanded offered a sense of constancy underpinning the incessant change of everyday life. Just as empty dining chairs between meals were absences waiting for the presence of their diners, so the shrine was imagined as a potent absence. The presence that it marked, however, was ultimately unfathomable. It was a totem of the mysterious nothingness which remained, for Heidegger, the constant companion of being and the primary locus of meaning. The shrine also marked – for better or worse – the rigid hierarchies of Catholicism, fixing age and gender roles among members of the family.

In the philosopher's model of architecture, these places were identified and understood according to the horizons of the individuals who dwelt there, both physical and imaginative. The recognition of these places was complex; some aspects were shared between residents, others were more individual. To Heidegger, these places with which the dwellers were intimately acquainted – some everyday, some attributed with more sacred qualities – located the residents with respect to being, and to the divinities. Such places offered, for him, a palpable sense of nearness. They allowed the dwellers to identify a centre, or maybe multiple centres, to their lives.

Heidegger claimed that the farmhouse both 'drafted' its inhabitants' occupation, and became a memorial to it. To him, the residents' dwelling was recorded over time in the fabric of the building and the paraphernalia of their lives placed there. For the philosopher, buildings are rich in insight, comprising a 'workshop of long experience and incessant practice' (1971, 161). To him, the configuration of a building reports physically the understanding involved in its construction and use. It offers tangible insights into the thoughts of its builders, should people choose to look for them (Gooding, Putnam, Smith 1997). In this model of architecture, buildings are memorials to the engagements of mind with place involved in their construction and alteration over time. Every structure bears the imprint of successive layers of dwelling. In Heidegger's scheme, as proposed through his description of the farmhouse, people remain constant participants in a game of architectural forensics. Every layer of paint, every drill mark, fitted hook or gouge in a wall is akin to the soot-blackened timbers or carved stones which provide archaeologists with clues. The Black Forest farmhouse, for Heidegger, manifested the everyday crafts of life in physical form. A long way from bookish philosophy, these crafts involved understanding garnered by individual human imaginations, through building and dwelling, from their engagement with the places around them. Heidegger implied, however, that the crafts of making and living carried meaning and had the authority of philosophy. To him, the conjoined activity of building and dwelling *is* thinking; the acts are associated together as a kind of extra-verbal philosophy.

In this model of architecture, buildings are memorials to the engagements of mind with place involved in their construction and alteration over time. Every structure bears the imprint of successive layers of dwelling.

The hypothetical farmhouse drew from other houses, suggested Heidegger. Its makers had learnt from construction tested by others, tapping the resource of buildings already made. They had no interest in the restless reinvention of form. By a dwelling 'that has been', he argued, the residents were 'able to build'. The farmhouse was made as a Heideggerian thing, and thus involved its occupants in 'a craft [. . .] sprung from dwelling'. To Heidegger, for people familiar with it, the house became a tool to help people make sense of the world around. Its places, appreciated through experience, became a frame of reference from which to explore outwards. Just as the bridge in 'Building Dwelling Thinking' renegotiated its site and the lives of its users, the dwellers constantly renegotiated the places of the farmhouse in association with the world around. To Heidegger, the house became a place as a physical marker, a part of the earth. It also became a place by siting human activity and offering itself as a tool for understanding.

It was the distinctive order of the farmhouse that arguably remained most important to Heidegger. This order resonates with the rituals and rites of passage, in the context of historical time, which characterised young Heidegger's life in Messkirch as a bell-ringer and chorister; when his days were scheduled by the calendar of feasts and festivals and by a succession of baptisms, weddings and funerals. The philosopher's farmhouse, however, doesn't so much accommodate the liturgy of Catholicism as the liturgy of everyday life. It was informed by Heidegger's stays at his mountain hut, where necessities of subsistence merged with the landscape and its seasons in routines of writing, living, eating and sleeping. At the Black Forest farm, for Heidegger, building and dwelling were to be found in self-sufficient unity, the fourfold a crucial partner in multiple identifications of place.

The farmhouse demonstrated the ethos that Heidegger advocated, manifesting the philosophical craft he found involved in everyday life. However, he argued that 'in no way [. . .] should or could [we] return to building such houses'. Acknowledging that the life the farmhouse stood for was gone, he advocated the reclamation of its order of building and dwelling in new ways which he left unspecified. To him, the house 'illustrates by a dwelling that *has been* how it was able to build.' It demonstrated the best alternative he knew to the prevailing technocratic model of architecture, obsessed with the production of buildings as art objects. Heidegger left to his audience any solutions for the reclamation of the farmhouse's order in contemporary life. He concluded [his emphases]:

> However hard and bitter, however hampering and threatening the lack of houses remains, the *real plight of dwelling* does not lie merely in a lack of houses [. . .] What if man's homelessness consisted in this, that man does not even think of the *real* plight of dwelling as *the* plight? Yet as soon as man gives thought to his homelessness, it is a misery no longer. Rightly considered and well kept in mind, it is the sole summons that *calls* mortals into their dwelling. (1971: 161)

This final flourish is a last demonstration, were it needed, of the moral dimension of 'Building Dwelling Thinking'. Building and dwelling were a matter of morality, and Heidegger perceived himself to be the moralist best able to determine their horizons.

Romantic provincialism

Heidegger's Black Forest farm is a striking example of his inclinations toward the romantic and archaic. His statement that the farmhouse's particular ethos had passed suggests he anticipated the charges of nostalgia which are easily levelled at it. Although Heidegger made clear that the order it described should be reclaimed anew, that order is certainly more at home with country ways than with city life.

The philosopher Albert Borgmann has written about what he calls provincialism and cosmopolitanism in Heidegger's writings (Borgmann 1992). Cosmopolitanism and provincialism describe attitudes to the world which are often considered in opposition. Advocates of both attitudes tend to caricature advocates of the other. Cosmopolitans tend to dismiss provincials as prone to exclusion: inbred, introvert, invidious, reliant upon romantic myth. Provincials dismiss cosmopolitans as deluded: bound-up in the priorities of fashions and systems, entranced by fickle obsessions with professionalism and expertise, setting themselves and their self-appointed heroes on false pedestals. Heidegger's romantic conception of the Black Forest farm clearly has provincial priorities. And we have seen that he was not averse to using the caricatures of cosmopolitanism in arguing against technocratic outlooks. While Borgmann calls the provincialism of 'Building Dwelling Thinking' 'critical and affirmative', the essay has been attacked by commentators who argue the case for cosmopolitan priorities.

One such critic is the architectural writer Neil Leach. Leach writes about Heidegger's provincialism:

> **Identity [. . .] becomes territorialised and mapped on to a geographic terrain. The individual becomes one with the land in a process of identification which is itself mythic [. . .] In this dissolving into nature, difference is suppressed and a new identity is forged with mother earth. Thus, we find constant references to natural phenomena – storms, blood and soil – in fascist ideology [. . .] It is precisely in the context of an identity rooted to the soil that those groups not rooted to the soil become excluded. (1998: 33)**

For Leach, the study of dwelling and place inevitably leads to questions of identity. He considers moments of Heidegger's writing which emphasise an affinity with particular places and argues that the notion of place implies a feeling of belonging which has fascist tendencies. To Leach, a group of individuals who have an affinity with a place might feel that they belong there. From this follows the possibility that others may be deemed not to belong, which can become intolerance to the stranger or foreigner. The extreme of belonging to a place can thus be seen as the persecution of perceived outsiders.

The extreme of belonging to a place can thus be seen as the persecution of perceived outsiders.

Leach also finds the romanticism of Heidegger's hypothetical farmhouse intolerant with respect to gender. Drawing from the work of Jean-François

Lyotard, Leach contrasts 'the myth of the *"domus"* ', the phenomenon of home, with a more alienated model of city life in a contemporary 'age of the megalopolis' (Lyotard 1991). This mythical image of home, according to Leach, suggests traditional domestic arrangements:

> **The domestic hierarchy of the *domus* likewise has its natural order, with the master and the mistress (the *dominus* and the *domina*) and the *ancilla* (the female servant). (Leach 1998, 34)**

For him, talking of home implies a mindset in which women are relegated to domestic servants. Indeed, as we've seen from the philosopher's association of men's work with engineering and women's work with spinning mills – supplemented by his reported remark after the 'Building Dwelling Thinking' debate at Darmstadt that home begins with marriage (Harries 1996, 106) – it is clear that the philosopher's thinking was hardly feminist.

Following Lyotard, Leach suggests that the domestic home, '*domus*', is a dangerous myth which tends toward the exclusion or exploitation of 'others' of many kinds, from women to those perceived as foreign. To Leach, its order is now lost: supplanted by the city, the 'megalopolis'. And with it, any sense of belonging is transferred from home and homeland to jobs and possessions. For him, this passing is not to be mourned but celebrated. In a characteristically cosmopolitan critique of provincialism, he equates place with home and domesticity and dismisses it as dangerously deceptive.

In the face of such charges, Heidegger's involvement with Nazism does not make the defence of his thinking about place any easier. Romanticism, as displayed in the provincial priorities of the Black Forest farm, cuts through Heidegger's writings about architecture. And while romantics may be indulged as dreamers in most cultures, romanticism is more problematic in a German context. It has been argued that a conjunction of writers into the early twentieth century, such as Friedrich Hölderlin, Johann Gottfried von Herder and Friedrich Nietzsche, opened up a special path to Nazism and established an intellectual space to be invaded by Hitler's genocidal rhetoric (Blackbourn and Eley 1984, 1–35). Certainly, romantic provincialism and its German sources loom large in Heidegger's writings not just during Nazism but also before and after. And it is writ particularly large in the example of the Black Forest farmhouse offered as a talisman for architecture. As Leach shows, Heidegger's work and his thinking on architecture are easily implicated.

'. . . Poetically, Man Dwells . . .'

The title of the last of the three texts explored here takes its title from a phrase of a Friedrich Hölderlin poem: '. . . poetically, Man dwells . . .' It is connected with its two contemporary essays but also remains distinct from them. Addressed to a literary audience, it is the most rhetorical of the three, least concerned with concrete examples. The text contributes to Heidegger's thinking on architecture by explaining how people 'measure' things around them and how they make sense of the world.

'. . . poetically, Man dwells . . .' was first given as a lecture at the elegant Bühler Hohe spa in the mountains above Baden Baden. Delivered on 6 October 1951, it was one of a series of Wednesday evening presentations by public figures in post-war German culture including Carl Orff, Emil Pretorius and Beda Allemann. The resort invited such visitors to entertain spa guests and literary townsfolk. Heidegger's text was published first in a 1954 edition of an academic journal, *Akzente: Zeitschrift für Dichtung* and reprinted in the book *Vorträge und Aufsätze* which also contained 'The Thing' and 'Building Dwelling Thinking'.

'. . . poetically, Man dwells . . .', or in German '. . . *dichterisch wohnet der Mensch . . .*', interprets phrases of Hölderlin's poem, working outwards from the line which Heidegger chose as the title. The German word '*Mensch*' is less gender-specific than the English word 'Man', closer to 'person'.

Heidegger felt that building and dwelling were always involved with attempts to make sense of existence, and were thus poetic.

Heidegger addressed the notion of poetry. For him, poetry was defined very broadly, describing all thoughtful human creations. Poetry was linked to building and dwelling – considered as a single spontaneous activity as in 'Building Dwelling Thinking' – from which it derived its authority. Heidegger felt that building and dwelling were always involved with attempts to make sense of existence, and were thus poetic. He felt that such attempts occurred properly, and poetically, through measuring: an activity which approached insight by judging experiences of human circumstances alongside each other. Rather than science, which Heidegger thought separated things out for investigation, the measuring that he advocated took place through a constitutive unity connecting people with things and the world. This unity was engaged with the fourfold preconditions of existence already discussed in 'The Thing' and 'Building Dwelling Thinking'. For Heidegger, in the unity of these preconditions, poetry and dwelling remained intense measures of one another, helping individuals make sense of their circumstances.

Poetic measuring

The term measuring appears in 'Building Dwelling Thinking' but Heidegger expanded on it in '. . . poetically, Man dwells . . .'. He began by questioning Hölderlin's statement '. . . poetically, Man dwells . . .', asking:

> How is 'man' [. . .] supposed to dwell poetically? Does not all dwelling remain incompatible with the poetic? (1971: 213)

Echoing the opening gambit of 'Building Dwelling Thinking', Heidegger argued that contemporary dwelling had been disturbed by the post-war housing crisis. He felt that that dwelling was distanced from poetry by popular perceptions of the frivolity of poets' work and by the 'literature industry' of publishing, whose emphasis on production he bemoaned (1971, 214). To Heidegger, the etymology of the Greek word for making – *poiesis* – linked poetry with dwelling. He implied that all making thus involved poetry to some extent. He also implied that poetry didn't necessarily have to involve words. Heidegger thus argued that poetry and dwelling weren't as incompatible was commonly assumed; rather that proper dwelling was primarily poetic.

Heidegger discussed language, advocating poetry as a special sort of language, suggesting that people misinterpret their relationship to it. For him, people assume in error that they control words. He felt that this wasn't the case. The power relationship was inverted. He argued: 'man acts as though he were the shaper and master of language, while in fact language remains the master of man' (1971, 215). Richard Polt notes that Heidegger challenged two commonly held assumptions with regard to language: first, that language is a tool for one person to communicate information to another; and second, that prosaic language is normal and more poetic language somehow strange and secondary (1999, 175). Heidegger felt that language exerted control over people, manipulating their possibilities for expression. For Heidegger, language was no neutral instrument. He urged a greater consciousness of the layers of meaning inscribed in daily conversation. Heidegger felt that poetry, as he defined it broadly, was a deep human involvement with the world. With its implicit suggestion of making, poetry
was not for him about expression but instead a distinctive listening to experiences of language and inhabitation.

. . . poetry inevitably linked the making involved in every individual's own building and dwelling to other acts of making throughout history, aligned ultimately with the creation of the world and its mythologies.

For Heidegger, 'poetry is what really lets us dwell' (1971, 215). He wrote about poetic building, claiming it as an ongoing activity rooted in individuals' receptive experiences of their circumstances; echoing the sense of order he derived from the Black Forest farmhouse. He considered poetry in relation to building and dwelling by expanding on the Hölderlin extract of the paper's title:

Full of merit, yet poetically, man
Dwells on this earth. (1971: 216)

The philosopher suggested that Hölderlin considered dwelling to be poetic despite the 'merits' of life's routine, finding it significant that man dwells 'on the earth'. This suggestion draws from the fourfold that Heidegger wrote about in the two essays explored above, although he didn't name it as such here. The philosopher suggested that Hölderlin had identified the character of distinctively poetic building for mortals by contrasting it with daily merits. To Heidegger, 'poetry is what first brings man on to the earth, making him belong to it, and thus brings him into dwelling' (1971, 218). For him, poetic making was an impetus at the core of the building and dwelling which he judged central to everyday human existence. Moreover, through its root in human making, the philosopher considered that such poetry inevitably linked the making involved in every individual's own building and dwelling to other acts of making throughout history, aligned ultimately with the creation of the world and its mythologies. Creation, in its most fundamental sense, was echoed for Heidegger in the creative act of making.

Heidegger worked towards a discussion of measuring by taking a larger extract from Hölderlin's poem:

> May, if life is sheer toil, a man
> Lift his eyes and say: so
> I too wish to be? Yes. As long as Kindness [*Freundlichkeit*],
> The Pure, still stays with his heart, man
> Not unhappily measures himself
> Against the godhead. Is God unknown?
> Is he manifest like the sky? I'd sooner
> Believe the latter. It's the measure of man [*Des Menschen Maaß ist's*].
> Full of merit, yet poetically, man
> Dwells on this earth. But no purer
> Is the shade of the starry night,
> If I might put it so, than
> Man, who's called an image of the godhead.
> Is there a measure on earth? There is
> None. (1971: 219–220)

The philosopher didn't analyse the whole extract, pursuing instead certain words and phrases. His selection from the poem notably contains the four elements of his fourfold: earth; sky; divinities ('the godhead'); and mortals ('man'). Heidegger concentrated upon aspects of the poem relevant to these constituents. Of particular importance was the realm 'measured out for the dwelling of man' between earth and sky (1971, 220). Heidegger connected the word 'measure' – which recurs three times in the Hölderlin extract – with the word 'geometry', advocating a particular conception of measuring as an activity rooted in poetic making.

Like his critiques of building production and the notion of object, Heidegger's measuring belonged with experience rather than science or mathematics:

> Measure-taking gauges the between, which brings the two, heaven and earth, to one another. This measure taking has its own *metron* and thus its own metric. (1971: 221)

The philosopher's discussion of measuring was another challenge to the mathematical abstraction which he found all too prevalent in contemporary society. Measuring wasn't primarily scientific for Heidegger. It didn't involve counting off mathematical intervals from a tape or a rod. It didn't involve any systematic application of frameworks derived from others. Instead, it is described by the German word for measuring, *messen*, which, although it also refers to mathematical gradation, carries connotations of comparing like with like. The basic elements of this comparative measuring, for Heidegger, were the fourfold preconditions of life that he identified. The activity involved a concentrated listening to what was around:

> A strange measure [. . .] certainly not a palpable stick or rod but in truth simpler to handle than they, provided our hands do not abruptly grasp but are guided by gestures befitting the measure here to be taken. This is done by a taking which at no time clutches the standard but rather takes it in a concentrated perception, a gathered taking-in that remains a listening. (1971: 223)

The philosopher argued that it was important not to set up abstract ideas as ideal standards, but instead to explore things and experiences in the context of other things and experiences. Heideggerian measuring involved listening. It could judge anything against anything. It might be done emotionally and instinctively, in a bodily and sensory way, or it could be more reflective and deliberate. The tools for measurement, in his scheme, were an individual's judgement, their imagination, their senses and emotions.

The tools for measurement, in his scheme, were an individual's judgement, their imagination, their senses and emotions.

Although there were different approaches to measuring, Heidegger felt that poetic measuring was distinctive because it implicated creation (1971, 224–225). Following his fascination with the very fact of human being, he judged that it was because of the mortal nature of human existence, as life towards death, that creation had special authority. To him, the primary impetus of poetry lay in human measuring of creation.

Heidegger's sympathisers often use closely observed examples, sometimes from literature, to illustrate the sort of measuring he advocated. Alphonso Lingis' account of a bed offers an example of bodily and sensory measuring:

> My bed was, the first night, crisp and brittle, foreign; little by little it has become intimate. It has acquired a very decided and very obvious fleshy texture; as I lie enveloped within it, I no longer distinguish where my body leaves off and where an alien surface begins. At first, I had that very vivid awareness of these sheets *touching* me, an alien surface *in contact* with the frontiers of myself. Little by little, this frontier fades, obliterates itself and becomes indefinite. The intimacy of the flesh diffuses throughout the whole bedsheet, finally into the bed itself, and the room also by a sort of contagion. They have become incorporated. (Lang 1989: 201–213)

In Heidegger's scheme, the individual might measure themselves against their bed and, in turn, measure the bed against themselves. The bed's dimensions and peculiarities are known instinctively by measure with the body. The individual might be said to feel at one with it. In its familiarity, this bed could also become somewhere of refuge, a personal territory that permits measure of the world. Lingis' account is similar to that of Georges Perec who writes in *Species of Spaces*:

> **The resurrected space of the bedroom is enough to bring back to life, to recall, to revive memories [. . .] The cosnesthetic certainty of my body in the bed, the topographical certainty of the bed in the room, these alone reactivate my memory, and give it an acuity and a precision that it hardly ever has otherwise. (1997: 21)**

Interpreted according to Heidegger's scheme, Perec here suggests that someone might measure other beds with their own. Their bed becomes a kind of Heideggerian measure. Their familiarity with it, and their knowledge and memories of it, might help them to test their perceived present against a past; against an imagined future; or against others who have slept there. Always associated with creation, for Heidegger, such earthly measurement opens contact with the ultimate mystery of life and could, possibly, help people to think differently about their place in the world. In Heidegger's scheme, individual and bed don't just measure each other but also the circumstances in which they're found. Individual and bed coalesce in measuring. This measuring may be instinctive and barely thought, or it may be more deliberate.

George Steiner writes about the more deliberate sort of Heideggerian measuring in his book *Real Presences* (1989). He begins with a speculation, imagining a world in which written secondary criticism of literature, music, art, philosophy and architecture (like this book) is banned. In its place, he would substitute other modes of criticism. He suggests that a novelist could narrate in criticism of another novel; that a musician might compose to criticise music; that a dancer may criticise a composition with the movements of their body. For Steiner, such commentary would be less self-referential than conventional journalistic or academic criticism (1989, 3–50). It springs from someone's creative alignment with others – positive or negative – thinking with them as part of a mutual making sense of the world. Steiner's hypothetical realm of criticism contradicts the model of research as a process of 'thesis', 'antithesis' and 'synthesis' established in contemporary research culture following Hegel's dialectical imagination (Taylor, 1975). Steiner, after Heidegger, suggests that there are dimensions beyond the scope of linear argument present in any attempt at making sense of the world through experience. In this scheme, reduction to linear argument is assumed to leave things out. Heidegger's notion of measuring belongs with Steiner's dancer who dances their commentary, or composer who comments in musical notation. Measuring is primarily poetic for the philosopher, which is to say that it springs from creativity worked through listening and making.

To Heidegger, when someone with poetic inclinations submits themselves to the world and deliberately or instinctively takes measure of its things and phenomena through creative acts, she or he creates poetry themselves.

To Heidegger, when someone with poetic inclinations submits themselves to the world and deliberately or instinctively takes measure of its things and phenomena through creative acts, she or he creates poetry themselves. For the philosopher, any outcome of this poetry also becomes a measure, added to a reservoir of human measures. Like the hypothetical bridge of 'Building Dwelling Thinking', it becomes something already there which helps people negotiate their place in the world. In Heidegger's scheme, such creations reflect the world and ask for responsible re-imagination. To him, they're made in human reflection and thus remain somehow special; even approaching the divine.

Making sense

For Heidegger, building and dwelling take place through measuring, which binds them together. Whether instinctive or more deliberate, such measuring is always conducted through immediate physical and imaginative experiences rather than through scientific experiment. For Heidegger, people primarily appreciate their surroundings – and particularly the buildings that they inhabit

– according to a creative interpretation of their experiences. Heidegger located this notion of measuring in a broader context. He proposed a distinctive model of how people make sense of the world.

In exploring 'The Thing' and 'Building Dwelling Thinking', we saw how Heidegger challenged what he felt was a contemporary tendency to parcel-up thinking into ideas, to set up ideal models supposedly distinct from day-to-day experience. Likewise, in '. . . poetically, Man dwells . . .' Heidegger stressed that measuring should happen in the context of a unity which binds life's experiences together with the things they measure, not by separating them. In one of his more challenging passages, he wrote:

> **The same never coincides with the equal, not even in the empty indifferent oneness of what is merely identical. The equal or identical always moves toward the absence of difference, so that everything may be reduced to a common denominator. The same, by contrast, is the belonging together of what differs, through a gathering by way of the difference. We can only say 'the same' if we think difference. It is in the carrying out and settling of differences that the gathering nature of sameness comes to light [. . .] The same gathers what is distinct into an original being-at-one. The equal, on the contrary, disperses them into the dull unity of mere conformity. Hölderlin, in his own way, knew of these relations. (1971: 218–219)**

Heidegger was playing with his literary audience in Baden Baden here, baffling them a little, engaging in his customary tactic of setting up complexities from which he could then present his own argument as clarification. His point isn't perhaps as confusing as it might first appear. We've already seen how Heidegger refuted the notion that ideas are somehow outside and above everyday human experience; how he preferred instead a phenomenological approach, suggesting that any thinker can only think from a condition of already existing on the earth. Heidegger's point in the paragraph above is made in this context. For the philosopher, individuals have to recognise enough difference between things so that they can measure other things with them. But, he argued, they should not separate them from everyday experience like science does, making them the object of dissection in a laboratory or analysing them as pure abstract ideas in a lecture theatre. This suggestion is clarified in the context of how Heidegger thought that people make sense.

Heidegger didn't believe that people make sense by arriving at a methodical outcome derived from meticulous analysis. For him, making sense is instead a moment of clarity, a smoulder of enlightenment that can't so much be described as experienced. Hans-Georg Gadamer, following Heidegger, describes such moments as 'evocations in which a striking word is found and an intuition flashes for a fleeting moment' (1994, 17). To Heidegger, making sense is a split second in which a jigsaw of thoughts click into place, the realisation of something new or a re-comprehension of something taken for granted. For him, these split second insights are part of a stitchwork of intuitions that comprise an individual's understanding.

Heidegger didn't believe that people make sense by arriving at a methodical outcome derived from meticulous analysis. For him, making sense is instead a moment of clarity, a smoulder of enlightenment that can't so much be described as experienced.

In his later writings, Heidegger's favourite analogy for this flash of insight of mysterious origin was a forest clearing. Introducing a collection of writings called *Pathmarks* (1998), or *Holzwege* in German, Heidegger likened making sense to walking on a forest path. This analogy made reference to a colloquial German expression *'auf dem Holzweg sein'*, 'to be on a wood-path', which is like the English expressions 'to be on the wrong track' or 'to be up a blind alley'. Being lost on a forest path, being lost in trying to make sense of something, is no problem for Heidegger, as George Steiner writes:

> It is our task, begins Heidegger, to set discussion on its way, to bring it 'onto a path.' The indefinite article is intended to underline the postulate

> that this path is only one among many, and that there is no *a priori*
> guarantee that it will lead us to our goal. It is Heidegger's constant strategy
> to show that the process of undertaking, the motion on the way, not only
> precedes the attainment of whatever goal we have set ourselves [. . .]
> but in some sense equals this goal in dignity and meaning. But although
> the path chosen will be one of many, it must lie inside the forest [. . .]
> It implies that there are other paths that lead *out* of the forest and thus
> *mislead.* (1992: 20–21)

For Heidegger, the scientific method of investigation which subjects an object to a system was alien to human experience; distant from the forest path. Findings which are derived from such systems, he implied, tend to say more about the systems themselves than what they aim to investigate. The scientific approach would, perhaps, be like exploring a forest by striking out according to a compass bearing. The compass suggests no attempt to understand how people have engaged with the forest intuitively before. Explorers don't first engage their own minds with the forest to try to understand it for themselves, but instead rely on an artificial instrument, trampling everything in their way to pursue the imposed route. To Heidegger, exploring by walking a forest path which was already there instead allowed the territory itself to guide exploration.

It's easy to feel lost on a forest path: the tree canopy is darkly enveloping and the dense lattice of trunks opens or closes distant views. The disoriented explorer follows their intuitions when walking; sometimes using paths well made by others, sometimes following forks that are less well trodden. In Heidegger's path metaphor, the clearing amongst trees was an elusive goal. When reached, its sunlight appears abundant in comparison with the forest and it permits a distant view, hinting at orientation. The German *Lichtung* describes a forest clearing but can also mean illumination, carrying connotations of enlightenment, of arrival at understanding. Arrival at the clearing, in Heidegger's analogy, was like the mysterious flash of realisation that meant reaching some kind of insight.

It was best to make sense of things by experiencing them in context, Heidegger argued, rather than separating them out for abstract experiments. The world and its things should be followed and listened to, navigated by intuition and judgement. To him, any insight would best be experienced as a flash of realisation in the context of a unity of thinking, rather than deduced through some spuriously methodical process with tendencies to separate rather than unify. For Heidegger, making sense involves individuals opening themselves – actively or passively – to the possibility of experiencing insight. And those insights are already present as latent possibilities in the world, ready to be found.

To him, any insight would best be experienced as a flash of realisation in the context of a unity of thinking, rather than deduced through some spuriously methodical process with tendencies to separate rather than unify.

Heidegger advocated a unifying sense of oneness (1971, 218–219). His thinking appears indebted to his explorations of Eastern thought, particularly that of Lao Tse (1989), and his studies of the mystic theologian Meister Eckhart (Davies, 1994). For Heidegger, the prevailing Western notion of the mind is as a detached intellect which makes distinctions; for example distinguishing the colour black from white. In contrast, for Heidegger after Lao Tse and Eckhart, oneness shows that black and white are indistinguishable from each other. Instead black, white and the many greys between are recognised as an inextricable totality. Rather than presuming to know white and testing blackness against it, white and black remain recognisably different but not self-sufficient. They couldn't exist without each other. They're part of the same totality from which individual parts can't be extricated and known in isolation. The human capacity to think about them is part of the same whole too. Thinking is always already there, around and within the people who are trying to make sense. In this scheme, separation is an alien idea. People don't measure by separating out. Rather, measuring happens in the context of oneness. Separation is unwelcome because it allows people to feel an artificial superiority over the world and over other humans, perhaps encouraging them towards inappropriate attempts at control.

For Heidegger, poetry as creative making resides in receptive human experiences of this binding oneness to which he felt people belong. For him, this model of making sense involves an integrated unity of world, mind and insight. It is a radical quietude which underpins the unifying physical, intellectual and temporal order that Heidegger claimed for the Black Forest farm in 'Building Dwelling Thinking'. Heideggerian identifications of place make sense of the world through measuring and oneness. Likewise, the conjoined activity of building and dwelling, for the philosopher, receives authority through a poetic receptiveness to the existing conditions of site, people and society.

Authenticity

At the end of '. . . poetically, Man dwells . . .' Heidegger claimed authenticity for his model of architecture. He related measuring to poetry in the context of building and dwelling:

> [. . .] dwelling only occurs when poetry comes to pass [. . .] as a taking of measure for all measuring [. . .] no mere gauging with ready-made measuring rods for the making of [plans]. Nor is poetry building in the sense of raising and fitting buildings. But poetry, as the proper gauging of the dimension of dwelling, is the primal form of building. Poetry first of all admits man's dwelling into its very nature [. . .] Poetry is the original admission of dwelling.
>
> The statement, *Man builds in that he dwells*, has now been given its proper sense. Man does not dwell in that he merely establishes his stay on the earth, beneath the sky, by raising growing things and simultaneously raising buildings. Man is capable of such building only if he already builds in the sense of the poetic taking of measure. Authentic building occurs so far as there are poets, such poets as take the measure for architecture [*für die Architektonik*], the structure of dwelling. (1971: 227)

Heidegger discussed 'architectonics', referring to humans' organisational structures for things. The word architecture is arguably used more often like this today than in the philosopher's time, for example in reference to the 'architecturing' of a computer program or a political agreement. To Heidegger, organisation is a creative act. Giving things organisational structure characterises poetry and inevitably displays the human measurement involved. For Heidegger, the broadly defined activity of poetry – which might refer to writing, making, building, music – involves the individual measuring themselves against their surroundings in an effort to make sense. In doing so, they sift, structure and align experiences. For him, the outcome of any poetic act displays these alignments to others. To him, poetic creation begins from every individual measuring themselves according to their circumstances and experiences. Where successful, and this is what distinguishes poetry from lesser creative activities for him, poetic acts will resonate with their beholder.

Arguably the most important point in this passage of '. . . poetically, Man dwells . . .' is contained in the last sentence: 'Authentic building occurs so far as there are poets, such poets as take the measure for architecture, the structure of dwelling'. Heidegger's claim for 'authentic' building and dwelling is significant. He categorised building and dwelling as good or bad according to whether or not it fitted his conception of poetry and poetic making; according to whether or not, in the terms of his philosophy, it was involved in creative attempts to make sense of the world by helping humans to measure the conditions of their existence. Good building and dwelling does this, for him, and bad building and dwelling does not. There is no room for any in-between. The polarising effect of Heidegger's claims to authenticity, in '. . . poetically, Man dwells . . .' and his other writings, remains arguably the most contentious aspect of his work. Such claims inspired one of the major criticisms directed at his writings: Theodor Adorno's book *The Jargon of Authenticity* (1986) first published in 1964.

The polarising effect of Heidegger's claims to authenticity, in '. . . poetically, Man dwells . . .' and his other writings, remains arguably the most contentious aspect of his work.

Adorno wrote in response to what he perceived to be the increasing influence of Heideggerian vocabulary in post-war Germany. As we've seen, Heidegger tried to attribute special significance to familiar terms by claiming unfamiliar meanings for them through his distinctive etymologies. Adorno began his book with reference to the nineteenth century philosopher Søren Kierkegaard's 'leap of faith'; a suggestion that religious faith relies on people not only pledging belief but being willing to rely on it, to jump the abyss certain of landing on the other side. To Adorno, Heidegger's vocabulary required a similar leap of faith. And, to him, it's unjustified. He described Heideggerian language as a cult (1986, 5). For him, the philosopher's jargon cloaked unsubstantiated argument with the 'pretence of deep human emotion' (1986, 6). Those who follow it do so rather like those who admire the emperor's new clothes. For Adorno, particular words are larded with pathos in an attempt to dupe the reader into belief.

It was the conjunction of Heidegger's authenticity claims with his way of speaking which Adorno found most problematic. He suggested that, while Heidegger's vocabulary claimed to validate the experiences of everyday life over ideal objects or ideas, it merely set up an alternative ideal which was just as distant from people. Influenced by the work of Karl Marx, Adorno felt that Heideggerian terminology relied upon, and was only capable of describing, a honeyed domesticity; like the Black Forest farm where agrarian subsistence was supposedly a constant and happy existence for successive generations. To him, Heidegger's vocabulary of ideal dwelling had no room for realities of poverty. It was incapable of expressing class-ridden inequality, its rosy expressions unable to deal with the privations of inequity and conflict. Especially in the post-war German context, Adorno worried that Heidegger's jargon all too easily allowed a middle-class belief in the normality of *petit bourgeois* domestic life; its authenticity claims admitting the suggestion that comfortable domesticity remained a safe and reliable constant in Germany before, during and after the Nazi era, a way of life temporarily interrupted by the unpleasantness of war (1986, 22). To him, Heidegger's vocabulary of authenticity validated and reinstated a romantic complacency. Worse, its polarising authenticity claims enabled a continuation of the fascist mindset.

Heidegger's sympathisers would dispute the links made between his etymologies and fascist ideology. Yet, the model of architecture summarised in '. . . poetically, Man dwells . . .' as 'authentic' poetic dwelling, which Heidegger also located in past manifestation in the Black Forest farmhouse, is clearly advocated without compromise. For him, authentic architecture subscribes to that model and inauthentic architecture does not. In the scheme of Adorno's critique, the ultimate authenticity claims are those of the Nazi racist policies which determined with murderous consequences who was 'authentic' and who wasn't. Any claim to authenticity, then, must raise powerful questions about who is given the authority to determine what is authentic, why and how. And human power relations – political, economic and social – which inevitably determine the outcomes must not be obscured with falsely comforting domesticity.

CHAPTER 5

Heidegger and Architects

Throughout his life, Heidegger sought contact with creative people who interested him, including writers, poets and artists. He took little interest, however, in seeking out architects or expert architecture. Heidegger visited Le Corbusier's new pilgrimage chapel at Ronchamp in 1953, not far across the French border from his Freiburg home, but the building didn't excite him. Instead he preferred to spend his time there following the Mass being said in an unusual way by a young priest (Petzet 1993, 207). An exception to Heidegger's ambivalence to meeting architects was his attempt to contact Alvar Aalto. The philosopher's biographer Heinrich Wiegand Petzet reports that, hearing Aalto kept the volume containing 'Building Dwelling Thinking' on his writing desk, Heidegger sent greetings. Attempts to broker a meeting were, however, ended by Aalto's death (1993, 188). Although Heidegger took little interest in architects and their work, plenty of architects in the latter part of the twentieth century showed interest in his writings. Architectural appropriations of his thinking are many and varied. I will focus here on one example which negotiates wider themes in the interpretations of Heidegger by architects and architectural commentators.

Heidegger visited Le Corbusier's new pilgrimage chapel at Ronchamp in 1953, not far across the French border from his Freiburg home, but the building didn't excite him.

Steamy waters

Peter Zumthor's architecture was made famous by a monograph published about his work in 1998, titled *Peter Zumthor Works: Buildings and Projects*. The introduction to that book discusses a quotation from Heidegger's 'Building

Dwelling Thinking', indicating the architect's knowledge of, and affinity with, the philosopher's writings. The most extraordinary building in the monograph is a spa built in the Alps, at Vals in the Swiss canton of Graubünden [see below], which Zumthor also discussed in an interview published in *arq: Architectural Research Quarterly* (Spier 2001). The Vals spa – famed among architects for its evocative sequence of spaces and its exquisite construction details – presents intriguing correspondences between Heidegger's writings and Zumthor's architecture.

Writing in his architectural manifesto, *Thinking Architecture*, Zumthor mirrors Heidegger's celebration of experience and emotion as measuring tools. A chapter titled 'A Way of Looking at Things' begins by describing a door handle:

> I used to take hold of it when I went into my aunt's garden. That door handle still seems to me like a special sign of entry into a world of different moods and smells. I remember the sound of gravel under my feet, the soft gleam of the waxed oak staircase, I can hear the heavy front door closing behind me as I walk along the dark corridor and enter the kitchen [. . .]. (1998: 9)

Zumthor emphasises sensory aspects of architectural experience. To him, the physicality of materials can involve an individual with the world, evoking experiences and texturing horizons of place through memory. He recalls places and things that he once measured out at his aunt's house through their sensual qualities. Here he echoes architectural practitioner and writer Juhani Pallasmaa who argues that, in a world where technologies operate so fast that sight is the only human sense which can keep pace, architecture should emphasise other senses which remain more immediately resonant (1996). Zumthor's Vals spa recounts the thinking he describes in his essay, making appeals to all the senses. The architect choreographed materials there according to their evocative qualities. Flamed and polished stone, chrome, brass, leather and velvet were deployed with care to enhance the inhabitant's sense of embodiment when clothed and naked. The touch, smell, and perhaps even taste, of these materials were orchestrated obsessively. The theatricality of steaming and bubbling water was enhanced by natural and artificial lighting, with murky darkness composed as intensely as light [see p. 94]. Materials were crafted and joined to enhance or suppress their apparent mass. Their sensory potential was relentlessly exploited.

Peter Zumthor's spa in the mountain landscape at Vals.

Water, light and shadow at Vals.

With these tactics, Zumthor aimed to celebrate the liturgy of bathing by evoking emotions. He said in his interview about Vals:

> They [the visitors] will recognise this building [. . .] because they know buildings like that on their Alps for the sheep and the cattle, which have this atmosphere [. . .] It's just simply building and surviving. They're the things you have to do [. . .].
>
> Ordinary people come in, older people come in and say it's good that I can come in here and it's not this cool atmosphere where I would like to wear a robe going into the water. In the bath there is a little bit of a mythological place, the drinking fountain where the water comes out. It has a red light and is purely an artificial, theatrical piece. It does have a tradition though. The old spas had these marble, shaped drinking fountains, so this is the new version but it is also a little bit theatrical. Also, coming down this long, long stair. This is like making an entrance, like in some movies or old hotels. Marlene Dietrich coming down a flight of stairs, or something. You make an entrance into the room. Also, the mahogany in the changing rooms looks a little bit sexy, like on an ocean liner or a little bit like a brothel for a second, perhaps. They are where you change from your ordinary clothes to go into this other atmosphere. The sensual quality is the most important, of course, that this architecture has these sensual qualities. (Spier 2001: 17, 22)

The word 'atmosphere' recurs in Zumthor's interview, and its plural is also the title of the architect's new book (2006). His preoccupation with this word suggests his concern to work outward from imagined experiences; to design by projecting what places should feel like based on his own memories of past places, trying to configure particular theatrical and phenomenal experiences in architectural form. Only once the qualities of prospective places emerge, for him, is building construction configured around them. Only then do the mathematically-scaled drawings of plan, section and detail acquire purpose. The measuring of body and mind – the navigation by intuition and judgement which for Heidegger makes sense in sparks of insight – becomes a way of designing for Zumthor, helping him imagine future places on the basis of remembered feelings. It also becomes the context within which he believes people will experience his architecture. Vals was conceived to appeal to sensual instincts first, and to interpretation and analysis second. For Zumthor, the spa should be tactile, colourful, even sexy to inhabit.

The measuring of body and mind – the navigation by intuition and judgement which for Heidegger makes sense in sparks of insight – becomes a way of designing for Zumthor, helping him imagine future places on the basis of remembered feelings.

Zumthor imagines experiences of the spa to be punctuated by things which evoke memories, which represent associations, like the drinking fountain or the stairs. He conceives of human endeavour in terms of traditions – and spatial representations of those traditions – locating things in what he considers to be their proper place in time and history. He also shares this tendency with Heidegger, who was anxious to locate his farmhouse dwellers according to rites and routines longer than a life. However, the architect's cultural sources are more cosmopolitan, also encompassing films and ocean liners which were clearly beyond the reach of eighteenth century Black Forest peasants. More recent traditions are admitted here, although they qualify only on the same terms as older ones; they have to seem simple, sensual, primary and elemental. The architect shares a sympathy for the mystical with Heidegger, claiming mythological qualities for moments in the spa. Like the philosopher, Zumthor also seems to aspire to an old ethos which preferred the immediate evidence of experience and memory over that of mathematical and statistical data.

It seems that, for Zumthor, the Vals spa achieves his design intentions by locating rituals of dwelling in place, with all the Heideggerian associations of those terms. By choreographing enclosure, mass, light, materials and surfaces, Zumthor hopes to set up conditions, like those surrounding the picnic discussed above, which encourage people to identify places through their bathing rituals, perhaps in association with their memories. He proposes a rich layering of place perceptions. And with another nod to Heidegger's Black Forest farm, the architect also considers place in terms of regional identity. In the interview quoted above, he evokes a simplicity that he finds in nearby Alpine buildings for sheep and cattle, rooting the spa in an agrarian view of the mountains associated with livestock and necessities of shelter.

Unlike Heidegger's Black Forest farmhouse or hypothetical bridge, Zumthor's spa was professionally procured. The eye of a trained designer – and the calculations of structural, acoustic, mechanical and electrical engineers, cost consultants and project managers – were brought to bear. Construction relied upon formal education and procurement procedures which, as we noted above, Heidegger felt were obstructions intervening between building and dwelling.

Zumthor's thinking at the Vals spa raises complex issues concerning the interpretation of Heidegger's thinking in architecture, including: the role of professional expertise; the notion of contemporary traditions; the notion that buildings and things can represent cultural meanings; the notion of regionalism; and the suggestion that design involves the choreography of experience. These themes aren't specific to this project and this architect; they characterise the writing and building of architects and architectural commentators sympathetic to Heidegger's writing over the last half century. They're worth developing in detail, both with respect to Zumthor at Vals and in relation to the writings and buildings of others.

Professional expertise

Zumthor seems aware of tensions between his sympathies for Heideggerian building, dwelling and measuring, and his participation in the structures of professional practice. In his interview about Vals, he said:

> It seems natural to say, OK, start with everything open – dark, light, silence, noise, and so on – that the beginning is open and the building, the design, tells you how these things have to be. Now [. . .] the world of building and construction is organised so that people can have nice vacations, and don't go bankrupt, so they can sleep well at night. They make these rules to take personal responsibility away from themselves.

This is true, this is how these building regulations come about. It's a matter of responsibility. (Spier 2001: 21)

Zumthor – in Heideggerian mode, and perhaps also with the American architect Louis Kahn in mind – advocated a piety of building: trying to develop a design in a way which lets it be what it wants to be, configuring physical fabric around real and imagined experiences. For him, statutory procedures disturb the instinctive relationship between architect, design and building. Set up by professionals for the benefit of professionals, regulations, he argued, alter design priorities. What Zumthor doesn't acknowledge, however, is his complicity in this situation as a fellow professional. For Heidegger, as we've noted, it's not just regulations but professionals themselves that are disruptive in Western societies: obstructing proper relations between building and dwelling; promoting buildings as products or as art objects. Zumthor attempts to reconcile Heideggerian building with architecture, whereas the philosopher would find the role of architects and the notion of architecture unhelpful. For Heidegger, Zumthor would be part of the problem, not part of the solution.

. . . statutory procedures disturb the instinctive relationship between architect, design and building. Set up by professionals for the benefit of professionals, regulations, he argued, alter design priorities.

Zumthor is by no means alone in seeking to reconcile Heidegger's thinking with professional architectural practice. A number of architects and architectural commentators have done so, tending to downplay the problems involved. It was primarily the writer Christian Norberg-Schulz who raised the profile of Heidegger's work in English speaking architectural culture – some years after the Darmstadt conference where the philosopher presented 'Building Dwelling Thinking' to architects – through his books *Existence, Space and Architecture* (1971), *Genius Loci: Toward a Phenomenology of Architecture* (1980) and *Architecture, Meaning and Place* (1988). For Norberg-Schulz, architecture presents an opportunity for people to achieve an 'existential foothold' in the world (1980, 5). To him, the contemporary practice of architecture involved fixing building and dwelling in place. He perceived inhabitation as a layer fitting over architecture like a glove over a hand. Norberg-Schulz implied that architecture and Heideggerian building were compatible, suggesting that an appreciation of Heidegger's work could help architects make their professional practice more humane and meaningful. Thus he provided a license which has been little questioned since, and architectural Heideggerians, broadly, have continued to relate the philosopher's thinking to professional practice in this way. They advocate that architects should be sensitive to non-expert building and dwelling, and make provision for inhabitants to engage in it. But, although they claim awareness of traditions of building and dwelling when designing, this singular activity is assumed to take place only once a building has been conceived and built according to conventional procedures. Unlike Heidegger's Black Forest farmhouse residents, who designed and built for themselves according to their own needs and cultural expectations, in this scenario the architect designs, contractors build, and only then do inhabitants build and dwell. Zumthor, it seems, approaches Heideggerian architecture in this way.

Another tradition of modern architecture

As described in his account of experience at Vals, Zumthor likes to perceive his architecture and its things in association with traditions, be they long standing or more recent. He shares this tendency with other Heideggerian architects and writers. The philosopher's work – not least in its etymologies, in its romanticism of routines and rites of passage, and in its insistence on authenticity – is imbued with a sense of historicity; a sense of the passage of time, of destiny, and of the past as a reservoir of thinking available to contemporary life. Traditions are often valorised by architectural Heideggerians following the philosopher's thinking; they are promoted as rich, operative histories for the present.

A few authors, notably Colin St John Wilson and Norberg-Schulz, have sought through their writings to assemble a tradition of recent architecture from particular modern architects and projects, with Heidegger's thinking part of their framework. They have sought to canonise, to institutionalise, an alternative history – or an alternative tradition – of modern architecture. Disregarding tensions between the philosopher's thinking and expert architectural practice discussed above, both authors invoked Heidegger in order to promote to architects what they considered a more humane modernism. Wilson began his post-war career designing housing with the London County Council, whose staff at that time included 'hard' modernists building Corbusian slab blocks and 'soft' modernists building low-rise suburban houses (Menin and Kite 2005). It was this latter, soft, modernism which Wilson, receptive to Heidegger's thinking on dwelling and place, set out to promote in *The Other Tradition of Modern Architecture* (1995), a book long in gestation. Wilson's architectural heroes included Alvar Aalto, Erik Gunnar Asplund, Hugo Häring, Hans Scharoun and Eileen Gray. His promotional tactic was to claim from these 'pioneer' modernists – by emphasising their sensitivity to site, dwelling, inhabitation and place – an authoritative tradition which should inform future practice (1995, 6–8). Wilson seems to have drawn from Norberg-Schulz who, writing fifteen years earlier, used similar tactics in concluding his book *Genius Loci* (1980), championing certain architects as exemplars of a Heideggerian architecture of place. Norberg-Schulz's list also included Aalto, and Frank Lloyd Wright, Louis Kahn, Reima Peitilä and Paulo Portughesi. Both commentators championed the form-making of such architects in response to site and inhabitation. And both writers thus claimed a Heideggerian tradition of modern architecture.

For Wilson and Norberg-Schulz, Heidegger's work, and the architects they ascribed to its orbit, suggested a point of resistance to hard modernism and postmodernism in architecture, an opportunity to condemn what they perceived as excessive design indulgence. They considered that they could promote to architects a more humane expert practice of modern architecture, which was sensitive to place and people, by canonising a particular tradition of architectural modernism and imbuing it with authority by association with Heidegger's philosophy. In consequence, many architects continue to associate Heidegger's thinking almost automatically with the list of 'modern pioneers' which Wilson and Norberg-Schulz valorised, which they set up in opposition to the architects of whose work they disapproved. There is a presumed equation widespread among architects: Heideggerian architecture equals this 'other tradition'. Peter Zumthor's name is often associated with this list. Whether he would concur is an open question. Traditions are, after all, determined by the people who promote and celebrate them.

Representation and meaning

Experiences of the spa at Vals should, for Zumthor, be punctuated by things which can call associations to mind: like the drinking fountain or the processional stair [see p. 102]. Such things, to him, conjure up memories for people. They do so by triggering associations with multiple traditions: from childhood games to Marlene Dietrich movies. The notion that architecture might have a representational role, evoking individual – and especially cultural – meanings, is also of interest to other architectural phenomenologists. Following Heidegger, writers have suggested that architecture had more representational power in the past; that it was once more involved with shared, meaningful traditions such as myths and religious stories. For these writers, the increasing influence of technology has, since the Enlightenment, both diminished such traditions and architecture's involvement with them, and has thus dulled possibilities for building to evoke meaning.

Following Heidegger, writers have suggested that architecture had more representational power in the past; that it was once more involved with shared, meaningful traditions such as myths and religious stories.

In *The Ethical Function of Architecture* (1997), Karsten Harries sought to reclaim a sense of meaning in architecture that he felt had been lost to scientific rationality. For Harries, ornament – in its broadest sense from ancient to modern – distinguishes architecture and has allowed access to meaning by reflecting stories about nature and the human appreciation of nature. He argued that, when its intelligibility is shared, such ornament has a poetic function that helps people to locate themselves with respect to place and community. For him, it

The processional stair from the changing rooms to the baths at Vals.

offers access to meaning and challenges the deadening rationality of technology. Citing Heidegger's Black Forest farmhouse – and largely disregarding criticisms levelled at it – Harries found authenticity in traditional architecture which manifests and represents the values of its builders who, for him, understood themselves as part of a community of like minds. He advocated the reclamation of this communal ethical responsibility for architecture, referring to ethics in the old sense of ethos, denoting shared values. For Harries, contemporary architectural projects are potentially revolutionary. In the face of technocratic rationality, they can offer opportunities for people, communities and societies to aspire to a more meaningful life by evoking associations and traditions of thought.

Historical shifts in Western conceptions of architecture have also been explored by Dalibor Vesely (2004), who has emphasised the representative possibilities of architecture. He considers the potential for buildings and places to manifest the values – the cosmologies – that give rise to their conception. Just as Heidegger thought that the Black Forest farmhouse manifested the attitudes of its builders, so architecture, for Vesely, can describe the thinking of the people and the society implicated in its construction. Like Harries, he explored what he considered to be tensions between instrumental and communicative, or technological and creative, roles of architecture. He argued that these roles have become divided; a split which is recorded, for example, in the respective professional roles of architects and engineers. Vesely traced the historical origin of this split to mediaeval optics and the development of perspective; to the first attempts to privilege a scientific description of light over immediate experiences of the qualities of vision. For him, although such technical descriptions have grown more prevalent and accrued more authority through history they remain inadequate. To him, these descriptions are merely simulations which are erroneously attributed more value than the realities they aim to describe. Vesely claimed that technical representations in architecture are divided in the contemporary world from the older ethical representations of shared meaning; from the associations with meaningful traditions also discussed by Harries. This division is a 'crisis of representation', claims Vesely, displacing meaning in architecture from human experience to the visual qualities of surface and appearance. For him, the job of architects in a contemporary context is to reclaim the communicative potential that architecture once had, to reconnect with its power to deal in meaningful experience. For Vesely, creativity remains the antidote to technology.

Unafraid to ascribe meaning and authenticity within a total theory of experience rooted in a particular historical sense of culture, Vesely and Harries claim a distinctive trajectory for the history of expert architecture: from a golden age predating the Enlightenment, when buildings were understood authentically through codes of shared meaning; to an increasingly technocratic world where the abstract and visual have become dominant. The levels of meaning that interest them most are primarily mythological and theological; elite historical traditions of Western culture which traditionalists would find more profound than the movies and childhood games cited by Zumthor. Nevertheless, Zumthor shares an interest with Harries and Vesely – derived at least in part from Heidegger – in architecture's potential to evoke associations and invite meaning.

Regionalism

Zumthor's claim for the regional credentials of the Vals spa has already been noted. He said in his interview about the building:

> All my buildings are sort of in a critical dialogue with the site, with the place. And maybe, ultimately, if you have a good result it's a nice metaphor to say that the building looks as if it has always been there because then, maybe then, you have reached some kind of rapport between the place and the building. At Vals this also has to do with hot springs and water, mountains and stone, things millions of years old. Stone and water, these images are close by. (Spier 2001: 16)

Stone and water are more than materials or phenomena for Zumthor; they're also intellectual notions, traditions of thought with a long history. They call to mind stories, among many others, about the translation of timber construction into stone in classical architecture, and the historical rituals of bathing in Turkish and Japanese cultures. Similar associative possibilities reside, for him, more broadly in stories about the traditions of a region, its history and its identity.

Perhaps cautious of charges of intolerance levelled at Heidegger's invocations of rootedness, Frampton did not seek to ascribe naturalness to any notional vernacular supposedly at one with land and people.

Critical regionalism in architecture was made famous by Kenneth Frampton after Heidegger, and has been discussed by Liane Lefaivre and Alexander Tzonis (2003). Frampton accepted Heidegger's arguments in 'Building Dwelling Thinking' about a loss of nearness. For him too, this loss provoked alienation in contemporary life, distancing people undesirably from a sense of place and belonging. Frampton argued in 'On Reading Heidegger' that architects should be responsible for place creation, at a small scale and in terms of locality, in order to recover a sense of meaning amid the decentring urbanism of late capitalism (1996). In 'Prospects for a Critical Regionalism' (1996), he argued that contemporary expert architecture should be more responsive to regional distinctiveness and possibilities for meaning available there, while nevertheless recognising that it can't be divorced from international culture and the homogenising tendencies of technology. Perhaps cautious of charges of intolerance levelled at Heidegger's invocations of rootedness, Frampton did not seek to ascribe naturalness to any notional vernacular supposedly at one with land and people. Instead, he explored the approaches to provincialism he located in the expert practices of architects such as Louis Kahn in Pennsylvania, Alvaro Siza y Viera in Oporto and Carlo Scarpa in Venice. Nevertheless, critical regionalism remains controversial because of its potential proximity to the fascist rhetoric of 'blood and soil'. Zumthor aligns himself with Frampton when he writes about a 'critical dialogue' between his designs and their sites, unafraid to claim meaning from locality.

Choreographing experience

Zumthor takes the choreography of experience very seriously in his design work, to the point where it affects his commercial relationships with clients:

Even if the clients are suffering [. . .] I insist on knowing something they have long forgotten or never known: that to do something well you need time [. . .] I mean, I need it because otherwise I cannot create an atmosphere, so what good would it do me to do a building which wouldn't have this atmosphere? I have to do it this way. I have this obsession because I feel the windows are important, and the doors, door hinges might be important, or all these things. So I have to be careful about these things otherwise I won't have this atmosphere and the whole objective of my work somehow would be gone. That's the way I work. (Spier 2001: 19)

Zumthor is not the first architect to obsess about designing in this way. Steven Holl's methods approximate to Zumthor's. Holl – whose published projects include the Stretto House, the Kiasma museum in Helsinki and Simmons Hall at MIT – has written about the influence of phenomenology on his thinking (Holl, Pallasmaa and Pérèz-Gomez, 1994) and he seems to owe a debt to Heidegger as well as to Gaston Bachelard (1969) and Maurice Merleau-Ponty (1989). Holl reputedly makes at least one watercolour sketch per day in order to explore the perceptual qualities of his projects, some of which are published in his book *Written in Water* (2002). He largely paints perspectives; a medium which, he feels, allows him to deal in the experience of architectural form more immediately than drawing in plan, section and elevation. Holl notes that working in this way requires him to think about form in light and shade. This technique becomes, for him, a means of choreographing experience. To Holl, painting is an intuitive act which opens up spontaneous and unintended design possibilities. Holl's paintings suggest that he differs from Zumthor though; that he is more preoccupied with the object qualities of his buildings, with shaping form externally, although still with intent to manipulate perception. His working methods encourage him to distort edges, contours and surfaces; dealing in light and shadow; anticipating transformations induced by rain, mist, sun and wind.

Aldo Van Eyck was another intense choreographer of architectural experiences. Van Eyck's biographer has connected him with Heidegger's thinking (Strauven 1998). His designs for post-war Amsterdam playgrounds, and his famous Orphanage and Mothers' House in the same city, contain a density of possibilities for children and adults to appropriate small places and identify with them. In this way, the projects appear somewhat Heideggerian. The architect seems to have been acutely attuned to possibilities for people to inhabit their surroundings. His playgrounds provided a series of things – varied floor textures, stepping stones, climbing frames, screens of different densities – waiting for children to inhabit them through their play. Children were invited to identify places in their games with these things, imagining new worlds around them. Van Eyck's bigger projects developed the thinking of the playgrounds into whole buildings. Edges were thickened to provide ledges, seats and shelves, offering places to settle and to put things down. Steps became seats and auditoria, sills became seats and ledges, shelves became hidey-holes and playscapes. Little openings, windows and fragments of mirror were introduced to enrich experience. These tactics allow for a density of place identifications in comparatively small spaces. They suggest uses rather than proscribing them, introducing a little ambiguity and redundancy so that individuals might use them in multiple ways. Van Eyck's architecture has been criticised because his prioritisation of human experience over object quality tends to favour the delightful fragment over the whole. Architects often consider his projects overworked, even tasteless, and it's easy to suspect that Zumthor wouldn't have much sympathy for them. Nevertheless, the two architects share a fondness for fragments which can stimulate experiences and evoke memories.

Steps became seats and auditoria, sills became seats and ledges, shelves became hidey-holes and playscapes. Little openings, windows and fragments of mirror were introduced to enrich experience.

Zumthor may also have little sympathy for the work of another famous choreographer of architectural experience: Hans Scharoun. While many of Zumthor's buildings champion the orthogonal, Scharoun's work is famed for its organic geometry. Scharoun attended Heidegger's talk at Darmstadt in 1951. The architect also made a presentation at the event, describing a hypothetical project for a school on a site near the conference venue. Peter Blundell-Jones has argued that Scharoun found an affirmation of his own ideas in Heidegger's talk (1997, 136).

Scharoun's plans show his preoccupation with breaking the rectilinear orthodoxy of four-square rooms in favour of more free-form enclosures designed around activities taking place there. The Darmstadt school project [see below] that he

Model of Hans Scharoun's Darmstadt school, showing street and classroom groups.

presented at the conference – which, although unbuilt, inspired his later school buildings – is a case in point (Blundell-Jones 1997, 136–140). Classrooms are collected in three age groups, each accessed through a gatehouse from an internal street. This street swelled and constricted along its length according to densities of use, variously acting as foyer, corridor or space to linger. It configured both prescriptive places and looser ones, suggested, as in Van Eyck's architecture, by changes in level, setbacks and ledges intended to foster informal contact. The lower-, middle- and upper-school classrooms each had their own geometries. Play and social skills were most important for the smallest children, and classrooms designed for them were introvert in character, facing south for bright sun and opening onto small gardens. Middle-school classrooms were designed for formal teaching, squarer and more serious, with an emphasis on cool reflected light and minimising distraction. Scharoun believed that older children were developing their own identity within a community and organised their classrooms in a less formal way with an outward focus. The configuration of the classrooms and classroom groups – also the school hall, gymnasium and library – each derived from the activities they were intended to house and the particular social geometries which happen when people gather, teach, learn, study and meet [see p. 110]. The whole school, in consequence, was an assembly of these parts, the street mediating between them. Scharoun's compositional abilities are evident in that neither the street nor the varied parts seem to suffer from their potentially awkward integration.

Scharoun's Darmstadt school, like many of Zumthor's projects, displays a particular Heideggerianism in its attention to atmospheres and moods, to site, and to changing qualities of light. It is also marked by Scharoun's concern to begin with social and political geometries of human gatherings, and a Van Eyck-ian preoccupation with architectural tactics that enable informal gatherings.

While the choreography of experience has been as important to Holl, Van Eyck and Scharoun as it remains to Zumthor, it has been expressed differently. These architects, like the writers with whom they have interests in common – Norberg-Schulz, Wilson, Harries, Vesely and Frampton – have been broadly sympathetic to Heidegger's notions of dwelling and place. A good deal of architectural commentary, however, is more critical.

Hans Scharoun's school at Marl, which drew from the Darmstadt school project, showing the 'break hall' street connecting classrooms.

In his interview about Vals, Zumthor downplays the activeness of his role in design. We've encountered his aspirations to piety and his attempts to enable an architectural idea to be what it wants to be. His aim of guiding projects towards a rapport with site and locality claims a similar modesty. The architect is keen to emphasise that he works instinctively with circumstances given to him:

> **It's hard to say where it comes from. I don't read too many books, architecture books, so it's hard to know where this comes from [. . .] it's not something intellectual I learnt. Somehow it's there, but don't ask me how. (Spier 2001: p23)**

Zumthor shares this attitude with Heidegger. The philosopher enthused about how philosophy found him at his mountain hut as a susceptible scribe. He also cultivated an anti-academic persona, arguing for the instinctive rather than learned dialogue, despite the obvious depths and breadths of his thinking. We've encountered criticisms of this studied passivity: Adorno's argument that Heidegger's vocabulary of receptiveness validated and reinstated a romantic complacency in post-war Germany; and Lyotard's and Leach's criticisms of his provincialist invocations of 'common sense'. The Heideggerian outlook which informs Zumthor's architecture is all too passive for many commentators. It militates against political activism.

Politics has become decisive to architectural interpretations of Heidegger's thought. By the 1990s, somewhat later in architecture than other academic disciplines, the philosopher's thinking had increasingly come under attack. It had previously been received largely sympathetically by the promoters of a Heideggerian 'other tradition of modern architecture', and the advocates of regionalism and representational thinking. However, Heidegger's problematic authenticity claims and the potential consequences of his romantic provincialism became more prominent in architectural debates about the merits of his model of building and dwelling. These disputes centred on the respective importance to architecture of phenomenology on the one hand and critical theory on the other.

Heidegger's problematic authenticity claims and the potential consequences of his romantic provincialism became more prominent in architectural debates about the merits of his model of building and dwelling.

It remains a common assumption among architects that these positions are more or less in opposition. To caricature, phenomenology (at least in its Heideggerian incarnations) champions the value of immediate human experience over scientific measurement and professional expertise, and tends to mythologize timelessness and situatedness. Critical theory, meanwhile, prioritises the political dimensions implicit or explicit in all human activities, and is opposed to monolithic claims of authenticity.

The umbrella of critical theory covers the work of disparate thinkers and groups whose work shares common threads, such as gender theorists, post-structuralists, post-colonialists, postmodernists, and deconstructionists (the latter understood differently beyond architecture). Impossible to summarise easily, critical theory has roots in Marxism, the writings of Adorno and the Frankfurt School, and French post-structuralism. Critical theory is also connected with Heidegger through Jacques Derrida's interest in his work on language (1989).

Heidegger's thinking, including that on architecture, is easily challenged from perspectives of critical theory. The philosopher perceived the 'essence' of building and dwelling in authentic attunement to being, unapologetic about the tendencies of essentialism and authenticity to exclude people. His writings display little fondness for what he saw as the human distractions of politics. The subsistence farmers of his hypothetical Black Forest smallholding were more involved with the passage of generations measured out in seasons than a struggle to right their class-ridden inequalities. Traditional heterosexual family roles were reinforced by the male domination of the community table in the farmhouse. The philosopher's suggestion that people should remain subservient to the forces of nature, attuned to mystical dimensions of making sense in oneness, downplays political involvement. Moreover, as noted with regard to criticism by Lyotard and Adorno, Heidegger's Nazi involvement becomes an overriding moral issue from perspectives of critical theory. Connections between the philosopher's thinking and Nazi ideology become decisive; and the facts of the case do not make it easier for Heideggerians to defend their man.

Although there have been moments of explicit conflict between phenomenology and critical theory in architecture – as we've seen with Lyotard and Leach – the debate has played out at least as much by implicit alignment. In an echo of the opposing tendencies of provincialism and cosmopolitanism discussed above, this debate has sometimes been polarised as a divide between conservative and liberal ideologies. Architects interested in phenomenology are cast as conservatives and those interested in critical theory are cast as liberals. This remains a widespread assumption, if largely unspoken, although it is inevitably caricature. The respective interests of both positions are not always mutually exclusive, nor have they always been incompatible.

Heidegger's work on architecture and, arguably, the architectural phenomenology which claimed him as a hero, has become a zero-sum game. Whatever it gives, its associations can also take away.

Debates at the time of writing have now moved on from the merits and problems of phenomenology in architecture. Any survey of the catalogues of Western architectural academic publishers and the online bibliographies of architectural theory courses, particularly in the US, demonstrate the institutional dominance of critical theory. Because of its fascist associations, Heidegger's work on architecture and, arguably, the architectural phenomenology which claimed him as a hero, has become a zero-sum game. Whatever it gives, its associations can also take away. Many architects and commentators have turned their backs on Heidegger in consequence although a few, including Zumthor, remain unswayed.

Imagination infected

Over the last half century, Heidegger's model of architecture has infected the imagination of numerous designers, historians and theorists. I find the infection analogy helpful. A mild infection is irritating but, in this, it can have positive effects as well as negative ones: it can disrupt someone's habits and force them to consider people and circumstances differently, to respond to them anew. Major infections, however, are debilitating. The sort of mild Heideggerian infection which, for example, always sees opportunities for small places in sills and thresholds like Aldo Van Eyck, or finds potential in designing around social geometries like Hans Scharoun, has some benefits. More pervasive conditions, however, can give serious cause for concern. Many, both Heideggerians and critics, have been sceptical of those who buy into the philosopher's vocabulary with little appreciation of its contexts; those who, as Gadamer suggested, do no more than metaphorically 'push around little ivory discs on which his terms are inscribed' (1994, 27). Jargon larded with pathos can only be irritating and pretentious. More importantly, the grave dangers of fully absorbed but uncritical Heideggerianism have been already been introduced here. Claims to authenticity – to any model of the world intolerant of others – should be resisted; as should invocations of the soil of place which are only a step away from illiberal politics and, ultimately, racism. Where Heidegger's romantic provincialism is absorbed uncritically, it can allow right-wing ideologies to flourish. Redneck Heideggerian infections must be challenged.

Tempting as this infection analogy is, however, it remains limited: arguably infection is received passively; a trial for the inflicted to bear. The key point I want to urge at the end of the book is this: if you engage with Heidegger's model of architecture then you should do it critically and actively. The philosopher's thinking is not offered here simply to be accepted without careful questioning. It remains difficult to appreciate a good deal of late twentieth century expert architecture and architectural criticism without some sense of Heidegger's thinking. Peter Zumthor continues to subscribe to it. But whether you choose to do so – and if so at what level of dose – must remain as much an issue for your political conscience as it does for your architectural judgement.

Further Reading

Heidegger's writings in German are being published as a complete edition of approximately 100 volumes – his *Gesamtausgabe* – incorporating changes and amendments that he made late in life (Sheehan 1980). English translations of numerous texts are available, not always mirroring the contents of German volumes and not always following the *Gesamtausgabe* plan. A full list of German titles and translations is available online at www.webcom.com/paf/hb/gesamt.html and an extensive listing of secondary literature on Heidegger in European languages (although only up to 1992) is maintained by The Albert Ludwigs University Freiburg at www.ub.uni-freiburg.de/referate/02/heidegger/heideggerkatalog.html (accessed 3 January 2007).

If you want to delve further into Heidegger's philosophy, plenty of general introductions are available. Richard Polt's *Heidegger: An Introduction* is particularly accessible, George Steiner's *Heidegger* remains thought provoking and Miguel De Beistgui's *The New Heidegger* concludes with brief overviews of the philosopher's reception within particular academic disciplines. A post-war text by Heidegger's student Karl Löwith – who, as a Jew, distanced himself from the philosopher during the Nazi era – remains a complex and intriguing introduction rich in nuance; it is translated as 'Heidegger: A Thinker in Destitute Times' in Richard Wolin's *Martin Heidegger and European Nihilism*.

Probably the best Heidegger biography is Hugo Ott's *Martin Heidegger: A Political Life*. Ott writes as an historian. He aimed to reflect the complexity of Heidegger's actions rather than his philosophical thought.

Edward Casey's *The Fate of Place* charts the history of the notion of place through philosophical history from the most ancient philosophers to the late twentieth century. It situates Heidegger's thinking in an extremely rich context, and offers an excellent survey of famous philosophers' work in relation to architecture.

Architectural phenomenology has drawn from Heidegger, but also from Maurice Merleau-Ponty and Gaston Bachelard. Untainted by Nazism, their *Phenomenology of Perception* and *Poetics of Space* respectively now tend to be the favoured sources of writers in this area. Both are challenging and can be rewarding.

A thoughtful overview of some challenges to Heidegger's thought in architecture was provided by Hilde Heynen in a 1993 article in *Archis* titled 'Worthy of Question: Heidegger's Role in Architectural Theory'. She helpfully reviewed the reception of the philosopher's work at that time in the context of wider theoretical issues. Themes she identified remain relevant.

Two fictional works have been considered as veiled critiques of Heidegger's biography in relation to his philosophy, both of which make good reading. Episodes in Günter Grass's *Dog Years* parody Heidegger and Heideggerian traits. Parallels have also between identified between Heidegger and the central character in Thomas Mann's *Doctor Faustus*, an intellectual who sells his soul to the devil.

Bibliography

Adorno, T. (1986) *The Jargon of Authenticity*, trans. by K. Tarnowski and F. Will, Routledge, London.

Alexander, C. (1977a) *The Timeless Way of Building*, OUP, Oxford.

—— *et al.* (1977b) *A Pattern Language: Towns, Buildings, Construction* OUP, Oxford.

Aristotle (1983) *Physics: Books III & IV*, trans. by E. Hussey, Clarendon Press, Oxford.

Arnold, D. (2002) *Reading Architectural History*, Routledge, London.

Bachelard, G. (1969) *The Poetics of Space*, trans. by Jolas, M., Beacon Press, Boston, MA.

Blackbourn, D. and G. Eley (1984) *The Peculiarities of* German *History*, OUP, Oxford.

Bloomer, K.C. and C. Moore (1977) *Body, Memory and Architecture*, Yale University Press, New Haven, CT.

Blundell-Jones, P. (1995) *Hans Scharoun*, Phaidon, London.

Borgmann, A. (1992) 'Cosmopolitanism and Provincialism: On Heidegger's Errors and Insights', *Philosophy Today*, no. 36,131–45.

Casey, E. (1997) *The Fate of Place: A Philosophical History*, University of California Press, London.

Conrads, U. *et al.* (1962) *Modern Architecture in Germany*, Architectural Press, London.

Davies, O. (1994) 'Introduction', in *Meister Eckhart: Selected Writings*, Penguin, London.

De Beistegui, M. (2005) *The New Heidegger*, London, Continuum.

Derrida, J. (1989) *Of Spirit: Heidegger and the Question*, trans. by G. Bennington and R. Bowlby, University of Chicago Press, London.

Frampton, K. (1996) 'On Reading Heidegger', in *Theorising a New Agenda for Architecture: An Anthology of Architectural Theory 1965–1995*, edited by C. Nesbitt, Princeton Architectural Press, New York, pp. 440–6.

—— (1996) 'Prospects for a Critical Regionalism', in *Theorising a New Agenda for Architecture: An Anthology of Architectural Theory 1965–1995,* edited by C. Nesbitt, Princeton Architectural Press, New York, pp. 468–82.

Frede, D. (1993) 'Heidegger and the Hermeneutic Turn', in *The Cambridge Companion to Heidegger*, edited by C. Guignon, CUP, Cambridge, pp. 42–69.

Gadamer, H.-G. (1994) *Heidegger's Ways*, trans. by J.W. Stanley, SUNY Press, Albany, NY.

Gooding, M., J. Putnam and T. Smith (1997) *Site Unseen: An Artist's Book*, EMH Arts/Eagle Graphics, London.

Grass, G. (1997) *Dog Years*, trans. by Mannheim, R., Minerva, London.

Harries, K. (1996) 'The Lessons of a Dream', in *Chora, Volume 2*, edited by A. Pérèz-Gomez and S. Parcell, McGill-Queen's University Press, Montreal.

—— (1997) *The Ethical Function of Architecture*, MIT Press, Cambridge, MA.

Heidegger, M. (1962) *Being and Time*, trans. by J. Macquarrie and R. Robinson, Harper and Row, New York.

—— (1971a) 'Building Dwelling Thinking', in *Poetry, Language, Thought*, trans. by A. Hofstadter, Harper & Row, London, pp. 143–61.

—— (1971b) '. . . poetically, Man dwells . . .', in *Poetry, Language, Thought*, trans. by A. Hofstadter, Harper & Row, London, pp. 211–29.

—— (1971c) 'The Origin of the Work of Art', in *Poetry, Language, Thought*, trans. by A. Hofstadter, Harper & Row, London, pp. 17–78.

—— (1971d) 'The Thing', in *Poetry, Language, Thought*, trans. by A. Hofstadter, Harper & Row, London, pp. 163–86.

—— (1973) 'Art and Space', trans. by C.H. Siebert, *Man and World*, no. 6, 3–8.

—— (1976) *The Piety of Thinking*, trans. by J.G. Hart and J.C. Maraldo, Indiana University Press, Bloomington.

—— (1981a) 'Why Do I Stay in the Provinces?', *in Heidegger: The Man and the Thinker*, edited and trans. by T. Sheehan, Precedent, Chicago, IL, pp. 27–8.

—— (1981b) 'The Pathway', in *Heidegger: The Man and the Thinker*, edited and trans. by T.F. O'Meara and T. Sheehan, Precedent, Chicago, IL, pp. 69–71.

—— (1985) 'The Rectorate 1933/34: Facts and Thoughts', trans. by K. Harries, in *Review of Metaphysics*, no. 38, 481–502.

—— (1992) 'The Self-Assertion of the German University' in *The Heidegger Controversy: A Critical Reader*, edited by R. Wolin, MIT Press, Cambridge, MA, pp. 29–39.

—— (1993a) 'What is Metaphysics?' in *Basic Writings*, edited and trans. by D. Farrell-Krell, Routledge, London, pp. 94–114.

—— (1993b) 'The End of Philosophy and the Task of Thinking' in *Basic Writings*, edited and trans. by D. Farrell-Krell, Routledge, London, pp. 431–49.

—— (1997) *Vorträge und Aufsätze*, Neske, Pfullingen.

—— (1998) *Pathmarks*, edited by W. Mc.Neill, CUP, Cambridge.

Heynen, H. (1993) 'Worthy of Question: Heidegger's Role in Architectural Theory', *Archis*, no. 12, 42–9.

Hofstadter, A. (1971) 'Introduction', in Heidegger, M., *Poetry, Language, Thought*, Harper & Row, London, pp. ix–xxii.

Holl, S. (2002) *Written in Water*, Lars Müller, Baden.

——, J. Palasmaa and A. Pérèz-Gomez (1994) 'Questions of Perception: Phenomenology of Architecture', *A&U Special Issue*, 7.

Hoy, D.C. (1993) 'Heidegger and the Hermeneutic Turn', in *The Cambridge Companion to Heidegger*, edited by C. Guignon, CUP, Cambridge, pp. 170–94.

Jacobs, J. (1961) *The Death and Life of Great American Cities*, Random House, New York.

Kisiel, T. (1993) *The Genesis of Heidegger's Being and Time*, University of California Press, Berkeley, CA.

Lang, R. (1989) 'The Dwelling Door: Towards a Phenomenology of Transition', in *Dwelling, Place and Environment*, edited by D. Seamon and R. Mugerauer, Columbia University Press, New York, pp. 201–13.

Le Corbusier (1954) *The Modulor: A Harmonious Measure to the Human Scale Universally Applicable to Architecture and Mechanics*, trans. by P. de Francia and A. Bostock, Faber & Faber, London.

Leach, N. (1998) 'The Dark Side of the *Domus*', *Journal of Architecture*, vol. 3, no. 1, pp. 31–42.

—— (2000) 'Forget Heidegger', *Scroope*, no. 12, pp. 28–32.

Lefaivre, L. and A. Tzonis (2003) *Critical Regionalism: Architecture and Identity in a Globalized World*, Prestel, Munich.

Lyotard, J-F., (1990) *Heidegger and the Jews* [sic], trans. by A. Michael and
M. Roberts, University of Minnesota Press, Minneapolis, MN.

—— (1991) *Phenomenology*, trans. by B. Beakley, SUNY, Albany, NY.

Löwith, K. (1994) *My Life in Germany Before and After 1933: A Report*,
trans. by E. King, Athlone, London.

—— (1995) 'Heidegger: A Thinker in Destitute Times', in *Martin Heidegger
and European Nihilism*, trans. by G. Steiner, edited by R. Wolin, University of
Columbia Press, New York, pp. 29–134.

Mann, T. (1949) *Doctor Faustus*, trans. by H.T. Lowe-Port, Secker & Warburg,
London.

May, R. (1996) *Heidegger's Hidden Sources: East Asian Influences on His Work*,
edited and trans. by G. Parkes, Routledge, London.

Menin, S. and S. Kite (2005) *An Architecture of Invitation: Colin St John Wilson*,
Ashgate, London.

Merlau-Ponty, M. (1989) *The Phenomenology of Perception*, trans. by C. Smith,
Routledge, London.

Norberg-Schulz, C. (1971) *Existence, Space and Architecture*, Studio Vista,
London.

—— (1980) *Genius Loci: Towards a Phenomenology of Architecture*, Academy,
London.

—— (1988) *Architecture, Meaning and Place: Selected Essays*, Rizzoli, New York.

Ott, H. (1993) *Martin Heidegger: A Political Life*, trans. by A. Blunden, Fontana,
London.

Pallasmaa, J. (1996) *Eyes of the Skin: Architecture and the Senses*, Academy,
London.

Perec, G. (1997) *Species of Spaces and Other Pieces*, Penguin, London.

Petzet, H.W. (1993) *Encounters and Dialogues with Martin Heidegger*,
trans. by P. Emad and K. Maly, University of Chicago Press, Chicago, IL.

Pevsner N. (1963) *An Outline of European Architecture*, Penguin,
Harmondsworth.

Polt, R. (1999) *Heidegger: An Introduction*, UCL Press, London.

Rudofsky, B. (1964) *Architecture Without Architects: An Introduction to
Non-pedigreed Architecture*, Doubleday, New York.

Safranski, R. (1998) *Martin Heidegger: Between Good and Evil*, trans. by
E. Osers, Harvard University Press, Cambridge, MA.

Seamon D. and R. Mugurauer (eds) (1989) *Dwelling, Place and Environment*, Columbia University Press, New York.

Seamon D. (ed.) (1993) Dwelling, Seeing and Designing: Toward a Phenomenological Ecology, SUNY, Albany, NY.

Sharr, A. (2006) *Heidegger's Hut*, MIT Press, Cambridge, MA.

Sheehan, T. (1980) 'Caveat Lector: The New Heidegger', *New York Review of Books*, 4 December 1980, pp. 39–41.

Spier, S. (2001) 'Place, Authorship and the Concrete: Three Conversations with Peter Zumthor', *arq*, vol. 5, no. 1, pp. 15–37.

Steiner, G. (1989) *Real Presences*, Faber & Faber, London.

—— (1992) *Heidegger*, Fontana, London.

Strauven, F. (1998) *Aldo Van Eyck: The Shape of Relativity*, Architectura and Natura, Amsterdam.

Taylor, C. (1975) *Hegel*, CUP, Cambridge.

Tse, Lao (1989) *Tao Te Ching*, trans. by R. Wilhelm and H.G. Ostwald, Penguin Arkana, London.

Unwin, S. (1997) *Analysing Architecture*, Routledge, London.

Vesely, D. (1985) *Architecture and the Conflict of Representation, AA Files*, n8, pp. 21–38

—— (2004) *Architecture in the Age of Divided Representation: The Question of Creativity in the Shadow of Production*, MIT Press, Cambridge, MA.

Wilson, C. St John (1995) *The Other Tradition of Modern Architecture: The Uncompleted Project*, Academy, London.

Wolin R. (2001) *Heidegger's Children: Hannah Arendt, Karl Löwith, Hans Jonas and Herbert Marcuse*, Princeton University Press, Princeton, NJ.

Zumthor, P. (1998a) *Peter Zumthor Works: Buildings and Projects 1979–1997*, Lars Müller, Baden.

—— (1998b) *Thinking Architecture*, Lars Müller, Baden.

—— (2006) *Atmospheres*, Birkhäuser, Basel.

[n.a] (1991), *Mensch und Raum: Das Darmstädter Gespräch 1951*, Vieweg, Braunschweig.

Index

Numbers in **bold** type indicate illustrations

existence 31; unconventionality of 33, 65
Frampton, Kenneth 105, 109
Frankfurt School 112

Gadamer, Hans-Georg 18, 36, 44, 84, 114
gathering 34
gender 75, 112
geometry 79; *see also* mathematics; science
German Democratic Republic *see* East Germany
German National Library 1
Gray, Eileen 100
Gropius, Walter 36

Häring, Hugo 100
Harries, Karsten 1, 101–3, 109
heaven *see* etymology; fourfold
Hegel, Georg 27, 82
Heidegger, Martin; biography 2, 15–20, 21–2; circular arguments 5, 18, 23, 37; and critical theory 112–14; critics of 1–2, 4, 88–9, 111–14; dislike of abstraction 4, 27, 37–8, 79–80, 83–5; disliked English language 51; engagement with architecture and architects 1, 3, 91; influence 1–2, 4, 88, 91–2, 105, 113–14; philosophy of and expert architecture, attempts to reconcile 98–9; reputation 1–2, 113–14; 'turn' 19–20; at Todtnauberg 6, 17–18, **18**, 20, 31, **65**, 66; as unconventional thinker 3–4, 33, 35; *see also* being; etymology; fourfold

'high' architecture 2–3
Hölderlin, Friedrich 19, 33, 74–5, 83; poetry 77–9
Holl, Steven 106, 109
Holzwege 6, 11, 84
horizons 6, 43, 49, 55–8
housing crisis, post-war 21, 36, 39, 42–3
human experience 2–3, 22, 26, 46, 97, 103, 107; mathematics and 58–62; phenomenology and 83, 112; place and 51–2; poetry and 87; science and 28, 58–62, 85
human history, buildings and 49
Husserl, Edmund 16, 17, 27

inhabitation 3
innocence 13
insight, sudden 84–5
instinct 4–5, 80–2, 98, 111

Jacobs, Jane 3
Jeanneret, Charles-Edouard *see* Le Corbusier
jug 25–6, 28–35, 48, 60
Jugendstil 36

Kahn, Louis 98, 100, 105
Kant, Immanuel 17
Kierkegaard, Søren 17, 89
Kisiel, Theodor 17

Lake District 6–14
landscape 6–14, 17, 33; bridges and 47; master of man 77
language 23, 25, 27, 76–7; personal language, fourfold as Heidegger's 33; *see also* etymology
Lao Tse 86; *see also Tao Te Ching*

post-structuralism *see* critical
 theory
pre-Socratic philosophers 19
Pretorius, Emil 75
professional architecture *see* expert
 architecture
provincialism 72–5, 105, 111–14

racism 13, 114; *see also* Nazism
religion *see* Christianity
Republic of Germany *see* West
 Germany
rhetoric 25
Riemerschmid, Richard 36
Rilke, Rainer Maria 19
romanticism 12–13, 72–5, 99,
 111–12; Nazism and 3, 13
Rudofsky, Bernard 3
ruin 10, 21
Ruskin, John 13

Safranski, Rüdiger 27
Scarpa, Carlo 105
Scharoun, Hans 1, 36, 100, 107, 109,
 114
Schopenhauer, Arthur 27
science 3, 60, 92, 103; inadequacy
 of 24, 33, 48, 61, 83–4,
 104
Seamon, David 52
secular society 17, 44
senses 7, 12, 80, 92–6, 103
shelter 10, 38–9, 44, 49
Siemensstadt 36
Siza y Viera, Alvaro 105
sky *see* etymology; fourfold
solitude 13
space, place and 51, 53, 56
spirit of place 1

Steiner, George 23, 33, 81–2,
 84–5
Stuttgart station 36
subsistence 44, 71, 89, 112

table, example of 41, 69; *see also*
 picnics
Tao Te Ching 25, 33
technocrats *see* science
technology *see* science

theology *see* Christianity
'Thing, The' 4, 21–2, 23–36, 63,
 83
things 23, 25, 28–31, 35, 46;
 buildings as 'built things' 23;
 and object 29; *see also*
 'The Thing'
thinking 7–8, 11; being and 27
Todtnauberg 6, 17–18, **18**, 20, 31,
 65, 66
totalitarianism *see* Nazism
tourism 13
Trakl, Georg 19
translation, difficulties of 51
travel 23
Turner, J.M.W. 13
Tzonis, Alexander 105

Unwin, Simon 53
urbanisation 3

Vals, spa at 5, 92–9, **93**, **94**, 101, **102**,
 104, 111
vernacular architecture 3, 42, 66
Vesely, Dalibor 1, 103–4, 109

Weber, Alfred 36
West German National Library 36